This book is about much more than the real estate industry. I am not in that field, but I am a retired business owner, so I totally felt and related to the things she has experienced on her journey. The way Denise unfolds all of her "Out of the Box" creativity, you can literally take her ideas and put them into any business setting. It's all about the consumer—period—regardless of what industry you are in. Her own personal stories keep you turning the pages until the end of the book. Her wit—and sometimes the embarrassing things she has done—make you reflect on the silly things you have done to entice customers in your own business. But rest assured, you will find something in the book you can implement in your business—and even in your personal life—immediately. I love her positive outlook on life, as the many things she has had to endure could make one just want to give up and quit. Her feisty attitude is one that says, "Never Quit—Ever" and believe me, I see it in the words she has written. What an inspiring story she has. Having this book is like having a friend who has been there and is now in your corner by sharing all her great ideas to make your business successful. Everyone needs a cheerleader in their life and Denise put it into a book for you to reflect on when you need a positive boost. Well done, Denise.

—Jayne Hall

Co-Founder of a Multi-Million Dollar Retail & Service Store in Oklahoma

OUT of the
BOX

My Response to Everyone Who Said
I Could Never Sell Real Estate

Denise Fawn Schroder

For My Husband & Soulmate,

Acknowledgments

Troy: You are my everything. God truly prepared my heart especially for you in His time. You have supported me, seen me and encouraged me to be the creative free-spirit that I am. (I know you being dragged into my social media shenanigans pushes you far out of your comfort zone.) For that, I am eternally grateful. You have entertained being pushed in front of the spotlight on mass stages when you are much more comfortable in the background playing a supporting role. We have grown and stretched ourselves together and taken the biggest and scariest leaps of our lives together. Thank you for accepting the strong woman that I am that craves to pave our own lanes. You are the love of a lifetime. You are God fearing and love me fiercely and unconditionally. You love me in all of my forms. It seems right now that all I've ever done in my life is make my way here to you. 13 years later and your eyes still melt my heart and I get butterflies every time you kiss me. Cheers to many more, the ride is just starting, and we've only just begun!

To my Family: Thank you for being genuinely happy for us. We have had some unwavering support from parents and my sister, Andrea. You have walked through fire with me and have been there as I rose from the ashes and rebuilt both myself and my life.

Connor and Jordyn: You have witnessed me and my life journey transforming for the good. My hope is you internalize that you too are capable of turning your life around and doing anything you set your mind to. I will be your biggest cheerleader and supporter always.

Mom: You live on through me every single day. I am honored to do my best to live beautifully and continue your legacy of serving others and making others feel immensely loved and special. Your guidance and influence on my life is infinite. You are the small voice I hear when I am still to this day struggling to make decisions. I carry your heart in my heart.

To Mo Anderson: You and Keller Williams have truly changed the trajectory of our lives. We have absolutely fallen in love with the culture of this company. You have been a constant source of bold inspiration pouring into our lives over the last 10 years. You have been ferociously generous with your resources, teachings, time and talents to help us all grow personally, spiritually and professionally. You and I are both farmers' daughters and that connection is so dear to me. I attribute that as one of the reasons my work ethic and faith are so strong. You are one of the most amazing people I have ever had the blessing to call a friend and a mentor. After tragically losing my Mom, it was so refreshing to send you an email about our next television appearances and each and every time you have ALWAYS taken the time to tell us how proud of us you are. I love who you are and what you stand for. You are so pivotal in Troy and I being able to live out our calling on our lives. You are an angel in my life!

To my Tribe of friends: Thank you for doing life with me. You have stood with me and for me through the darkest and brightest times in my life. You have always embraced my unique, quirky personality and sense of humor and for this I am grateful. At times, I hid behind humor and self-deprecation to make it through. Today, I have forgiven myself and others and I've gone on to live a joyful existence in Christ. Heidi and Julie, you have been a constant in my life. Thank you for choosing me no matter what season of life I was in.

To my brokerage, coaches and mentors (Keller Williams, Cyndi Carfrey, Jim Fischetti, Vija Williams, Adelina Rotar) I am forever indebted for the tough love, the unshakeable belief in us and veracity. When we wanted to quit or started to fall, you were each there to walk with us, pull us up and push us forward. You prayed for us and mercifully believed in us when we did not yet believe in ourselves.

To Jesse Cole: Your book The Yellow Tux and your entire organization is an inspiration to me. I connected with your thought process of not only doing things differently in business but the way in which you lead with such a faithful servant's heart. Having a "we" over "me" mentality is everything. Putting others first and seeing others succeed is true success.

To my Life Group: We do life together, I have grown more spiritually and personally than ever before. I love the relationships we have built, and we are genuinely tethered together through the good and bad. Kevin, you are our Pastor. You have poured into my heart, soul and mind. I am forever changed through your ministry.

40-Day Publishing: Dan, Darlene and the team have been nothing short of amazing. They have been with me every step of the way in producing this book. This is more than an item on my bucket list, it is a conviction that has come to full fruition. When Darlene asked me to speak at a Women's event, she told me she is a highly acclaimed author and owns a publishing company. She told me after hearing me speak, she wanted to read my manuscript that was sitting dusty in a google folder. Someone else had read it and I felt discouraged and fearful to share it. But I did it, I pressed send and the rest is history. Thank you for bringing this book to life and making it a reality.

I have always gravitated toward my own path. I have never in my life wanted to be "normal." God graced me with creativity and an innovative heart and mind. Be true to who you are and embrace your God given talents.

"I thought not fitting in was something I had to fix. Now I see it as my superpower." – Maxime Lagacé

To anyone that has ever felt like they were not enough, not seen or just too different to fit in. You are never too broken to be fixed. I encourage you to allow failure to be your biggest teacher, not a grave digger. If you have lost your identity or your path in life, it is never too late to refresh your path and not only grow from your failures, but courageously stand in them and share your story to become a lighthouse for others. YOU ARE ENOUGH!

Foreword

Denise Schroder is a force to be reckoned with.

When Denise Schroder walked into our event, I wasn't sure what we were in for. Her resume was impressive, and I knew she was successful, but I still didn't know what she might bring to the women sitting in front of her...the ones who desperately wanted to be successful in both their personal and professional lives.

She'd been on major network shows such as Steve Harvey, The Oprah Show, The Rachel Ray Show, and The Talk. I had asked her to speak for a women's networking group I was hosting. We had a little back and forth on Messenger but as we all know, it's hard to really connect with someone via messaging. Within five minutes of chatting with her face to face, I knew this woman was genuine and cared for people in a real, tangible way—especially women who needed to see examples of success up close and personal.

Denise didn't hold anything back. She was transparent. The women in that room needed to hear she had encountered real pain, real heartache on her climb to living a fulfilled and successful life. They needed to see she didn't always have it "all together." She'd been broken and hurt—in some ways, more so than anyone sitting before her—and she overcame and persevered.

Denise isn't just a client. She isn't just an acquaintance. She's become a dear, trusted friend who brings so much to the business world. Her intention in writing this book was to encourage other realtors. However, the ideas on these pages will serve any business owner who wants to think outside the box while taking their business to the next level. Her ideas are sound, applicable—sometimes a little zany—but I promise they will get you thinking.

Denise has a unique way of approaching social media. She not only stays in her lane, but first, she created the lane! She generously shares how she has used the power of storytelling to attract the attention of major networks, newspaper publications, podcasts, teachers, event holders needing public speakers, and national real estate publications. She has been recognized as an expert on a multitude of topics on major network shows such as Steve Harvey, The Oprah Show, The Rachel Ray Show, & The Talk. She is also not afraid to be self-deprecating. Her most recent appearance on national television was on Season 20— Worst Cooks in America on Food Network.

Denise gives freely in this valuable, content-filled, idea generating, thought provoking, and creativity inducing book so many principles for business owners to set in motion today. She and her husband Troy have reigned in the top tier of real estate production in the Oklahoma City Metro area for the past 10 years.

She isn't just a pretty face; she is also beautiful on the inside. We connected immediately and I'll forever be better for knowing her.

—Darlene Shortridge

CEO and Co-Founder 40 Day Publishing

Contents

Introduction

You will never make it.

No one will ever love you.

You don't have what it takes.

You can't stand out.

You are worthless.

You aren't enough.

This was the twisted soundtrack that was on constant replay inside my head.

I am certainly not trying to be a complete Debbie Downer, this is just me spilling a little tea. This was a soundtrack on replay in my head for years and years. Finally, I had had enough. I needed to arrest this undying insecurity within myself. I knew God had a bigger, more joyful and fulfilling calling on my life. I was tired and exhausted. I had two choices: carry a chip on my shoulder about some horrendous cards I had been dealt over the course of my life or choose to be a fighter. I laid my victim mentality behind. I deployed a search and rescue team on myself. I realized we can't always wear out our welcome hosting pity parties or wait for someone to throw a lifesaving raft or jump in to swim and save us. I made a choice and that was to rescue myself. That choice saved me and has helped me create a life I never knew I could have, much less deserve. More importantly, it has helped me understand that every battle I went through allows me to be a lighthouse for others. I can now illustrate that you can take charge of your life and use it for good, helping others realize their worth and calling. Everything you have clawed your way through, ever waded through, climbed through, sobbed through, prayed through is setting the foundation and structure to step into your very BEST SEASON.

Let's start at the beginning.

I am a true testament to never underestimating where you will find love. Who needs a cheesy dating app, right? I fell head over heels for my FEDEX guy. He sauntered into my office nearly every day for five years before our first date! He had a 1000-watt, Julia Roberts smile, beautiful, kind eyes, and the sexiest pair of legs I have ever seen. I would literally spring up out of my chair and do everything but scream, "Let me sign for the package." Once we had our first date, the rest was history! Little did I know my entire destiny and trajectory of my love life and career was about to change. There was something magical about our union. I felt like I had loved him for 1000 years, and we quickly became so fierce together, a force to be reckoned with. Twelve years prior to writing this book, we blended five teenagers and eventually went on to both quit our jobs the same day, December 3, 2010, to become self-employed! What a leap of faith! I never could have taken that leap without Troy. He was the yin to my yang, my partner in crime. But more than that, he allowed me the freedom to truly be who I am. He embraced my creative quirks, ideas, and catch-up dreams. Who knew he would end up being the love of my life, someone I locked arms with in the pursuit of a common goal, playing catch up and relentlessly chasing our dreams together.

TO THIS DAY, TROY IS THE GREATEST PACKAGE I HAVE
EVER RECEIVED!

THE WAY I LOOKED AT HIM ON OUR WEDDING DAY IS THE SAME TODAY. HE WAS WORTH THE WAIT.

Our journey to becoming self-employed was not glamorous. There were a lot of naysayers when we quit those jobs. Have you ever heard the saying "Bet the Farm"? Well, we DID! We had seven mouths to feed and $30,000 in savings to make this happen! Looking back in retrospect, $30,000 was NOT very much money to have in reserve. My plan was to start producing profit so quickly we never had to even touch the savings. Boy, was I wrong!

We had gotten into financial services. Troy had a long-time friend who was mentoring us. He expressed his success and sold us on a company that was a great fit, it seemed. Troy and I both got our Life Insurance licenses and eventually our Health Insurance licensure. Shortly after we quit our jobs, we found out the mentor was going under financially and was not thriving as he had led us to believe. His false words had given us the boost of confidence to take the leap of faith in the first place!

I thought the only thing more depressing than going and sitting in people's homes to talk about death was actually being a mortician. When we decided that we really did not want to be in financial services, we were determined NOT to fail. We did not even tell our five kids that we were going to go another route. We were willing to do anything not to go back to a J-O-B, but more importantly, we refused to admit we might have made a grave error in taking the jump to build our own empire.

We bought precious metals for a while. Do you remember when gold and silver prices skyrocketed to an all-time high of around 1900 a troy ounce? We transitioned into the precious metal business right then. Remember when you saw Cash for Gold on every corner? Literally, every corner. It was more saturated than the real estate market now! We did very well for about nine months.

After the price of precious metals plummeted, we got connected with a roofing company and thought it was the "dream." They would set our appointments and all we had to do was go sell a roof. We assessed the roofs, after which our main goal was to get a contract. The majority of the time we were sent on a wild goose chase, sometimes an hour or more from our home, doing nothing but wasting gas, not to mention our sanity and self-esteem. We got several contracts by door knocking. And by door knocking, I mean walking door to door randomly with four-inch heels on, in the hundred-degree Oklahoma heat, praying someone would allow us to assess their roof. I felt I was nothing more than a glorified Kirby vacuum salesperson. The only difference was I did not get to pour dirt on someone's floor to prove I had the perfect way to clean it up. Instead, I had to beg to get on their roof. And, just to be clear, if someone's roof is not falling in or leaking, they do not think they need your help. I was at a pretty low point when we were selling roofs.

Actually, let's be real, I was depressed, frustrated, and feeling hopeless. But it got even lower when the company we were working with was not honoring our commissions earned. In essence, they were royally messing us over, which in my mind equaled taking food off the table for our five kids. So, that relationship ended before we had worked any longer for free. You tend to wonder how people sleep at night messing others over like this, people who are just trying to make an honest living to care for their families. In retrospect, it was a huge learning experience; BBB ratings don't always mean people are honest and stand by a stellar code of ethics.

One day Troy came home from having breakfast with a friend who had done real estate. I had wanted to get my real estate license twenty-three years earlier after having some success in property management. I was discouraged and told I could never make it in such a saturated industry, and at best it would only be an expensive hobby. There was such a strong case presented to me, I was convinced that I simply did not have what it took to stand out to be able to find success. This time though, we were determined, and failure was NOT an option. The most beautiful thing of all is I used that negative seed of thought that I could never make it, planted years before, to propel our team by using social media in a creative, authentic way and build an organic brand and voice like no other.

It was not easy as we did not have a paycheck for seven months and had to live on savings with five mouths to feed. After seven months of tiresome seed planting, we sold forty homes in the first year. We now average over one hundred home sales a year with just the two of us. Overcoming the fear of quitting the jobs proved to be the best decision of our lives. Not only have we been able to succeed at a high level, but we have also been barrier breakers and disruptors in the industry. Our authentic, organic marketing approach to stay top of mind coupled with delivering stellar service quickly catapulted us to the top.

We have a national conference every year at our Keller Williams Realty Family Reunion. Our first year, I was asked to be on a panel. To say this was a BIG deal is an understatement. Out of 100,000 agents at the time, I was blown away at the opportunity. My arms should have been bruised because I pinched myself repeatedly to ensure I was awake. I can remember being interviewed for my intake by one of the top agents in the nation, Mark Spain. He would facilitate the interview at the conference. I was one of four agents that would be questioned for an hour in front of a massive audience. The three other agents do about $80 million a year in production. I felt naked, like a fish out of water sitting next to them. The class was called Marketing for Less. We are from Oklahoma, one of the cheapest places in the country to live. Even though we had sold forty homes in seven months our first year, which equaled about $6.4 million. I can remember Mark Spain saying to me that the focus is not the volume, that is all relative. You add value because you are creating marketing to be featured in the press, and selling forty homes in your first year with nearly no marketing cost incurred is astounding. We continue to run a lean marketing budget due to the organic ways we are able to reach our audience. Our perfect recipe uses humor and a business model focused on stopping the scroll, creating a presence and brand for staying top of mind in all things real estate. I have continued to stay in touch with the agents on my panel. What is nuts is they were curious about my methods of marketing effectively and I was star struck by their production and notoriety. That experience taught me so much. We can all learn from one another. We all have a different perspective, and it is refreshing to be inspired by someone, no matter if they are new or highly seasoned. We pride ourselves in being a constant student, always learning and striving to be better.

I was finally getting to live out my calling and my "why" in an unimaginable way.

THIS WAS A MOMENT; I KNEW I WAS ROOTED IN MY CALLING EXACTLY WHERE GOD WANTED ME TO BE.

ing with the Better Business Bureau and is fully insured, licensed, and bonded. Serving residen-

www.dahlheatandair.com.
Dahl Heat & Air is located at 829 W. Main in Yukon.

Local realtor selected for national panel

■ Schroder to attend 'Family Reunion' in Phoenix

Yukon realtor **Denise Schroder**, of the Schroder Group, has been selected among 96,000 people to be on an interview panel for the annual "Family Reunion" in Phoenix, Ariz.

Denise has the opportunity to teach and share on her area of expertise and passion, which is marketing.

Denise will speak on the panel Feb. 16, and some 10,000 fellow worldwide Keller Williams agents will attend. Family Reunion is the industry's most powerful training event.

Denise Schroder obtained her real estate license in August 2012. The Schroder Group has since catapulted at lightning speed to top 3% in production among all 3,300 Oklahoma City-metro realtors.

Being chosen to speak on a panel is an incredible

honor and the elite are chosen. To qualify as a panelist, one must have a certain level of production level and a valuable expertise.

The Schroder Group closed out 2013 with $6.4 million in production with their average-days-on-market being 15 compared to the OKC average of 72 days on market.

"I am humbled at the opportunity to be chosen for such an honor," Denise Schroder said. "I am looking forward to sharing Troy and my aggressive marketing strategies we use to get homes sold quickly as well as for top dollar. I am excited to be in the company of such highly esteemed Mega agents."

Denise's husband, lifetime Yukon resident **Troy Schroder**, is part of the Schroder Group.

Troy and Denise Schroder

mbers'
th "All
first in
Meet.

WHO NEEDS YOUR NAME IN LIGHTS? SEE YOUR STORY
FEATURED IN PRINT IS SO POWERFUL TOO!

Chapter 1
My WHY

I literally lived decades on autopilot. I was either in self-preservation mode or full-on survival mode. It all starts with the WHY! My "why" was getting through the next challenge or battle and taking care of my kids minute by minute. When I finally trudged through some of the hardest times in my life, I was able to not only find, but rediscover and reinvent myself. It is a slow and continual muscle build. When I broke my leg falling down a flight of stairs, I had to rebuild the strength and muscle in my entire leg. My orthopedic doctor had to remind me that I am not a superhero, and I would have to give my body a chance to heal before catapulting into rebuilding. The same is true in so many of our personal circumstances. You notice I don't refer to them as tragedies or with any negative connotation. The blessings from these circumstances have forced me to reevaluate, redirect energy, and pivot when I was getting in my own way. It was not easy. I had been in such a dark, vulnerable, weak, and broken state for so long. I reprogrammed myself to get rid of the negative self-talk, developed new thinking patterns, broke free from the chains of old habits, and surrounded myself with positive people. I found myself. At first, I did not recognize her. I had to peel back so many layers to get to who I am. That included reviewing and working through past traumas that were buried deep within. The woman I found was not the girl that was once broken, shattered, afraid, and spilled out on the cold floor. The woman I found had more grit, determination, drive, and a fierce perseverance to propel myself into something great. I did not want to just be strong, I wanted to be Ford tough! The woman I had become knew her value and would not settle, even if that meant being alone. I had always known I was meant to do more in this world than I was doing. All the years that I went through hell have brought me to the place I am today. The defeats, trials, failures, and mistakes led me up the ladder to be a more qualified person, to pour into others and give hope where it is void. My struggles have breathed a sense of life into me and are a constant reminder of the warrior I have become. All the obscurity and hopelessness I experienced gives me the deepest empathy to care, serve, and fiercely walk with others through the darkest of days.

"There is nothing stronger than a broken woman who has rebuilt herself." -Hannah Gadsby

My "why" went from surviving and just making it through the day to thriving. My "why" first and foremost is about being hypersensitive to being used to making a difference in the lives of others. In doing that as I go throughout every day, I in turn am blessed immeasurably. Our business has grown in unrealistic and unexplainable ways. The supremely unique opportunities I have experienced simply don't make sense. I had to change my mindset of asking myself, "Why me, God? Why am I going through these terrible things?" I changed my thought process to, "What am I supposed to be learning? What lessons are you teaching me to make me stronger, and better yet, to be used as an instrument to help others?" Now my mindset is truly one of gratitude for those times I could barely get out of bed or put my feet on the floor. This was a game changer. The absolute most profound events in my life came on the other side of sheer and utter terror!

My "why" is to be able to be independent if, God forbid, something happens to my husband, Troy. I also want to have financial freedom, and to whom much is given, much is required. Real estate has been the vehicle through which we have been able to achieve financial freedom with little overhead and in such a short time. I want to give to the organizations that break my heart. Breaking my heart for what breaks His is something I have heard in church and from my mom growing up. Giving myself permission to not feel guilty about being prosperous has been a journey. I was always used to being less fortunate than many others and felt mediocre when I was just inside a box I was dying to break out of. I did not just have a ceiling, for years I felt claustrophobic, locked in a box with no key or way of escape.

When you know your WHY, you don't work for your own rewards, you serve others. No matter how directionally challenged you are, your GPS is much easier to navigate when you are being propelled by an inner purpose. You are passionate and driven without apology. When you stretch your bandwidth to know your strengths, you are exhilarated and energized, and you have an endless amount of energy in reserve to serve. There is power in purpose driven passion. Living out your WHY positions you to be ferocious in pursuit of your crusade and to not be goal oriented, but mission minded. Changing my mindset to asking why I am put on this earth to make a difference and impact on others shifts things into a very self-aware and selfless existence. Changing my mindset to believing that I am put on this earth to make a difference, to impact others, shifts myself into a self-aware and selfless existence. When you architect your life around serving others, you will be blessed tenfold. Architecting building your "why" will naturally instill a fire in your belly. If you have a mission and have just lost your way a little bit, no worries. The beautiful thing is you can always relight your pilot light and get back on track or pave a new road altogether.

What is your WHY?

What excites you and your body physically reacts to it?

What creates a fire in your belly?

What would you do even if you did not get paid for it?

What are your innate strengths?

Chapter 2
Live to Leave a Legacy

Sometimes we lose perspective and lose sight of what is important. We can get all wrapped up, engulfed in the day-to-day operations of kids' schedules, cooking meals, soccer/dance practice, running our businesses, and putting out fires personally and professionally. There is so much societal pressure to have it all and do it all. Jesse Cole, of *Find Your Yellow Tux*, opened his book with his obituary. I thought it was amazing! Morbid as it may sound, putting pen to paper on what you want to be remembered for, what you stand for, and ultimately what your legacy will be is what will change the game. We get so caught up in our day-to-day hustles and just getting by that our purpose can get buried by the to-do lists and being in survival mode. Shortly after I read the opening to Jesse Cole's book with his obituary, my friend Jacque Calico's Facebook post said she was given an assignment to write her own obituary for a college course. I love writing and giving words of affirmation, so I wrote one for her and shared it with her.

I wrote, "Jacque Jones-Calico is an absolute ray of sunshine. She has a smile that lights up a room, a contagious laugh, and an overwhelming presence that commands every room she enters. She is always the first one to clap when others win and the first to get on her knees to mourn with those in pain or need. She has a giving spirit and has an infectious energy that magnetizes others to want to do life with her. She is a kind, compassionate, driven overcomer. She loves hard and dreams BIG. The world won't be the same without this pure soul. We will remember her smile, her warmth, her energy, her love for life, family, and friends, but also her gift with children, students, colleagues, and clients, many of whom over time also became friends. She worked very hard all her life, up until the very end. She made a difference in the lives of many, and her legacy is one of hope and relentless pursuit to serve others selflessly. Join us for the celebration of her life as a tribute to those who were blessed enough to call her friend."

Writing this obituary for my sweet friend caused me to do some heavy self-reflection. What would others say about you? I love these defining moments that can literally stop you in your tracks. We need pattern interrupters in our lives to get back on track and put things in a prioritized perspective.

I challenge you to take a few minutes and really think about, not only what you want to be remembered for, but what you want to instill in everyone around you. My mother's legacy is one I proudly accept the responsibility to carry on. I actually wrote this post for Mother's Day a few days ago. You can see my mother's legacy was loving big and fiercely. She focused on beauty from the inside being the most important. What is your core mission in life that you want others to carry on when you are no longer with us? Write a few sentences about how you want to be remembered and put it somewhere you read often. Focus on living out those principles and others will be truly blessed.

DENISE FAWN SCHRODER

MY GORGEOUS MOTHER

This throwback to 1981 reminds me of my beautiful mom on special days when I can't pick up the phone to call her. She would wear fancy nightgowns every night. She always looked like a million bucks but taught me you could do so while being smart and frugal. My mom did not focus on telling my sister and I we were pretty very often while we were growing up. She would compliment our hearts, intentions, attitude, inner beauty, tenacity, drive, character, our spirit, and who we were becoming. Never have I felt more beautiful than when my mother would say she was proud of me. This was one of the greatest gifts she gave me. Countless Mother's Days without her never get easier but I will never forget the valuable things she instilled in me and how she made me feel. What an incredible legacy! I am immensely grateful for the time I did have. She definitely lives on through my sister and me.

After losing my own mother when she was barely fifty, I gained a whole new perspective on life. I'd had to wrap my brain around the misdiagnosis of a hernia that was actually colon cancer, leading to medical tragedies that ultimately ended in her death. I survived this tragic loss and trauma because the fire inside me truly burned brighter than the fire around me. Don't wait to make amends with those you love. Tomorrow is definitely not guaranteed. Make the call, send the text, have a fierce conversation, forgive, and move forward.

When you have a vision and mission statement you live and walk by, it allows you to hyperfocus and frame a life by design to create a legacy for others. There are many free tools and templates online if you are stumped. We started the process of writing the words that represented our values, and what actions we needed to take to create a legacy, not just a successful business. This was a fun exercise and was eye-opening. We did it as a team!

Wordle is an awesome tool to create your power words from your vision and mission content. Display this word collage to help remind you who you are and to walk in harmony with your mission statement daily.

A vision statement is more than a few words tethered together to form a complete sentence. It is a commitment, an inward statement to all who are a part of your organization. For us that means all of our vendors who we allow to be an extension of our business must be like-minded and aligned with our values. Our vision is simple: Serve like you are chosen! Sounds so simple. But it is a huge commitment and responsibility in every word we speak/type or action we take. Serving as though you are chosen is a tall order! We don't always wake up on the right side of the bed, we have a headache, we had an argument with our spouse or teenager, a deal just busted at no fault of our own. The list goes on... We understand that every interaction, email, conversation, and action/inaction is sending a profound statement to our clients. When a client calls the office and the person answering the phone does not answer enthusiastically, the caller will assume they're being dismissed, that the person answering sees them as a burden or a hindrance to getting other things done. It's far better to answer with the attitude of being ready, willing, and able to serve them like you've been "chosen" to help them in this moment. We are in a competitive and cutthroat business. We have to earn the right for our clients to choose us, first and foremost. We want to be an advocate and for them to know, without a shadow of a doubt, we are all in this together!

Schroder Group Mission Statement:

We are a hungry, creative, innovative organization that challenges and nurtures both personal and professional growth. We measure our success by building others at the highest level. We are passionate about creating an environment where there are no ceilings and absolutely no dreams, goals, or aspirations too BIG! We are relentless in our pursuit to provide the most elite level of systems, standards, and performance. We tailor the customer service experience to leave a lasting impression and create raving fans for life. We strive to exceed expectations, always put the customer first, and lead with a servant's heart. The culmination of all these things creates opportunities to be prosperous in our greatest goal, which is making a difference.

When we know who we are, where we are going, and what our vision and mission is, we can live out our purpose in unimaginable ways. Drilling down on this vision statement and mission in your business is so powerful. I look back at mine often to remind myself why we do what we do. It should be posted in your office! It is not just a page in your operations manual, it is a daily reminder why we do what we do. You will definitely have days in your business you need to recalibrate and go back to your "why," your vision, and your mission.

Determining our purpose can seem overwhelming and daunting. Here are some easy questions to ask yourself, then sit in a quiet place and listen to that small voice.

What is important to me?

What is not important to me? (What are you spending time, effort, and energy on that is draining your tank?)

What do I want out of life?

What do I stand for?

What message do I want to convey?

What do we want people to say about us when we are gone from this earth? What is the legacy we'll leave? The beneficiaries of your legacy are anyone you make an impact on, and anyone you make a difference for. It is not just the person on paper who gets monetary gain that benefits from the legacy you build and ultimately leave to live on beyond your departure from this earth.

Chapter 3
It Only Takes One

I was adopted by my stepfather who raised me as his own from the time I was five. My biological father has never really been a part of my life consistently. And when he was, it was all at my instigation. Eventually even that was reduced, as I realized I had to consider the confusion it was likely going to cause my children to have a parental figure step in and out of their lives continually. Thus, referring to Dan as a stepfather seems foreign and just categorically wrong. He is my dad, in every sense of the word. He gave me such a gift. I had seen my mother struggle as a single mom, tirelessly working two jobs and not understanding her worth. He treated my mom like a princess from day one, gave me a feeling of acceptance, a sense of belonging, and encouraged me to be *me*. This is something I can never repay him for doing. His parents even became my loving grandparents, and he played a pivotal role in who I am today. He was my mother's One.

I always joke that my daughter helped jumpstart our real estate career into motion. Our youngest daughter, Jordyn, had just become friends with such a sweet girl, Lilli. Jordyn suggested to Lilli, who in turn suggested to her parents to have us list their home. Don't ever underestimate the power of a twelve-year-old with their parents! They had bought their dream lot in an incredible neighborhood in Yukon. They had attempted to sell their home over an eighteen-month period with two different real estate agents to no avail. Angel, Lilli's mother, called us and set up an appointment. I remember being so incredibly nervous, while at the same time, gleefully doing the happy dance all over my house. There was a lot at stake! Here is this family who desperately wanted to sell and move forward in their lives, depending on us to be nothing less than heroic. They hired us on the spot. We had the listing appointment and they never even asked us if we had ever sold a home before. I was in shock at how much they could see our contagious passion and determination.

We adrenalized the mission, and we were relentless in our pursuit to sell this home. We had the sellers pre-pack and de-clutter some things so it showed optimally online, and had new professional photography done. I can remember going door to door inviting neighbors to the Open House and doing a Broker's Open to get the realtor's attention. For eighteen months, this house was not selling. We needed to find a diagnosis of why and we had no experience other than extensive training, classroom time, and an overabundance of tenacity and drive. Their desperate situation with this house was literally in our hands and on our shoulders. Failure was not an option. After extreme efforts of door knocking, throwing a Broker's Open, and me dancing at the entrance doing human advertising to pack the Open House with the right buyers, we made it happen! We sold the home in two days with multiple offers, during a snowstorm in the winter, and I could not have been more excited!

Angel went on to refer us to an endless network of people, from her professional sphere of influence to her tight-knit church family. She has referred us to some of the most treasured friends we have. We have even flipped a house with one of her referrals and in turn refer them to a ton of construction professionals needing work. Angel is an interior designer, so I have always recommended her. When we did our first HGTV House Hunters episode, we recommended Angel to design the house for the buyer and her work was featured. Over the years we have reciprocated in such a beautiful way.

One way I have been able to show my deep appreciation is offering Angel business and mentorship coaching. She is the classic client, oozing with talent, just needing direction and empowerment on developing a social media brand and strategy. The latest idea is for her to offer herself as the perfect gift. In my industry, giving an experience is a genius gift. I am so tired of giving out Lowe's gift card or a cheesy, fake-grass, Oklahoma-shaped welcome mat. I want to give something that will leave a lasting impression. The concept is to give a tangible luxuriously wrapped gift box. Inside the box is a stunning card stock insert. Angel is at your disposal for two hours for only $50. YES, $50 to have a college-degreed interior designer come brainstorm with you. She will come to your home and help you hang photos, rearrange furniture, choose paint or accessory colors, or edit and repurpose items in your home already. Alternatively, she will meet you at a decor store and help you hand select furniture or accessory items. This is an experience our clients are raving about. Angel is a like-minded person we are so proud to have as an extension of our name and business. I have been able to help her get exposure in massive ways.

Our real estate office had a mandatory meeting. I asked my broker if I could have Angel and her display set up at the entrance. We had a drawing set up, the gift box displayed on the table, and we stopped the agents as they came in to explain "Designer in a Box." I was then able to refer her to a publication for the top 500 realtors in our area for some reasonable advertising rates. I asked the publisher if he would be open to also doing a video with Angel to explain the experience she is offering. It is so different from anything I have ever seen. Angel has been a huge connector in our business. I have always wanted to show her our immense gratitude in believing in us when no one else had. Being able to reciprocate and help her grow her business is so much more satisfying than a sale.

If I have already given a "Designer in a Box" gift to someone, I will ask if they would like another consultation experience with Angel. If I need another closing or appreciation gift, I like to offer something the person won't soon forget.

ANGEL, DESIGNER IN A BOX

These two are great ideas to solve pain points. The struggle is real in keeping our cars clean. We are also always busy and with that comes tension, so offering the mobile detailing or massage is an excellent option.

MOBILE DETAILING CAR WASH- You can hire someone to come to your client and wash and detail their car at their home.

MASSAGE- No one does not like to be pampered. You can offer your clients a couples' massage or a simple chair massage to extend some de-stressing remedies.

A way to the heart is through the stomach.

We were asked to dinner, as we commonly are after closing. The buyers love to show us all their improvements and how they have made the house their home. We went to dinner at Erin and Nathan's. Erin had recently started a baking business as a side hustle to teaching school. I brainstormed for a couple of days, and we turned our dinner into a mastermind for ideas to build her brand and gain traction in capturing business. It is so fun to watch her acting on these suggestions. Just this weekend, a local restaurant is going to put her bunchkins on the menu! We recently went to a local diner and her bunchkins are featured in their dessert case display. This made my heart so happy! Use your gifts to help your clients build and grow their endeavors. You will hear me repeat this often so there is no chance of you missing it. When you help others grow, I am certain you will be monumentally blessed.

We have a friend from church who is an impeccable painter. He painted our cabinets white. He is OCD and a perfectionist. These are traits you want in your painter! When his business slowed down, he called and asked if we knew of anyone needing work. I was able to use connections in all my private realtor groups, as well as post for thousands of people to view a before-and-after photo of the work he did in our kitchen. He told me that a few short hours later his phone started blowing up with requests for bids and possible jobs. THIS is what it is about! I was tickled pink to be able to help someone out that needed work. He is great at what he does, dependable, like-minded, and someone I am willing to attach my name to.

This last week, an incredibly talented tile guy we have used for years asked if we could try to drum him up some business. I immediately asked him to send me some fresh before-and-after photos of his work and references. I was then able to create a post and blast it to thousands of realtors in private groups to immediately get his phone to start ringing!

Who can you help right now to grow their business?

What are some simple opportunities you have to give a shout out or do a quick video testimonial that could impact someone else in a big way?

Make it your mission to always express to all your vendors you want to be their go to resource for ideas and help when they are struggling in their business. You certainly want to be able to pay it forward and bless them in this way going above and beyond.

If you are feeling discouraged, remember it only took one client to believe in us and it spread like wildfire!

Angel was my One–the first person to truly give us a chance when she was in a state of frustration and defeat!

It is so much more gratifying to give than to receive. When you give freely to help others, expecting nothing in return, the fruits come back to you tenfold. And…it only takes one!

Chapter 4
The Power of Having a Coach and Mentor

We have all most likely had teachers and coaches in some capacity our entire lives. The mentality that we don't need a coach once we reach the age of majority is just crazy. Some of the most impactful and influential humans in my life have been teachers and coaches. Why? Because they first believed in me, oftentimes, before I even believed in myself. They taught me fundamentals and basic skills to give me confidence, whether it was mathematics, learning to dance, or how to land a free throw. They also genuinely cared about me and were brutally honest, challenging me to always level up. The lesson that we can always improve our skills is one that is anchored deep inside of me. A coach can help you become clear on your vision and take you from where you are to where you aspire to be. They can hold your hand, help guide you, hold you accountable at a high level, and mastermind with you to take you to the next level.

When we first started with Keller Williams at the end of 2012, we had a team leader coach, Jim, and a productivity coach, Cyndi. Cyndi patiently taught us the fundamentals and was there with arms positioned to catch us and push us back up when we often felt discouraged and wanted to quit. Our team leader and coach, Jim, was a man I was deathly afraid of, at first. I have a very social, people-pleasing, gregarious personality. He is a very focused, serious, intentional person who takes no excuses. There are no reasons, no fluff or sugarcoating, just results. I remember he used to wear the same uniform every day: a black shirt, black pants, and black socks and shoes. He said the least interesting thing about him should be his attire. Picking out what to wear took time and energy. Simplifying his wardrobe meant others did not focus on what he was wearing, but on him, instead.

When you set your goals, they should petrify you. They should make you sweat! A good, healthy bit of anxiety with a powerful goal goes a long way.

Our goal was set when both of us quit our jobs the same day. Holy cow, talk about a lofty goal and a dream that made me sweat. We were betting the farm and taking a massive risk. We were making a wager on ourselves, and we knew it may not be easy. We wanted the American Dream so badly, it propelled us into a relentless pursuit. Having a coach and mentor to sit down with us and help us develop goals was key. You want to stretch yourself and not put a ceiling on your potential, while also being realistic. A coach will help provide this balance.

Our first year, we did not close our first transaction for seven months. Yes, seven months! That was 210 nights I went to bed praying if this was not what I was meant to be doing with my life, please show me a sign and quick! I was so confused about why I had waited two decades to pursue my calling and now our production seemed flatlined. Seven months of living off what was at the time a scarce savings account I never dreamt we would have to drain. We had five very perceptive teenagers who were watching every move we made with eagle-eye vision. We went to every educational class, every coaching session, door knocked every neighborhood, called everyone and their brother to tell them we are now selling real estate, hosted Open Houses every week, and still no sales. We were following instructions to a "t," and nothing was coming to fruition. Let me repeat that...NOTHING was coming to fruition. Until the last five months of the year, when it EXPLODED--- we sold forty homes. All the seed planting and nurturing finally became tangibly prosperous. I will never forget sitting in the office with Coach Jim. Troy and I walked into the office to go over our end-of-year production. Our chests were puffed up and we were feeling so incredibly proud. We were just waiting for a pat on the back. Heck, I wanted him to crown me with a tiara and shoot off a confetti cannon for all we had accomplished and endured.

He looked at us and very quietly and calmly said, "If you do this five years in a row, I will be impressed." He went on to tell us anyone can have a good year. He then drew out a graph on some white paper and walked us through how, if we stayed on track and never became complacent, we could be millionaires.

This man was so very wise, and he gave us a gift that day. He taught us early on we must have a vision and a mission statement that was more than a plaque on the wall. For him to look at us and believe in us in that way was a game changer. Initially I was crushed because we did not receive more praise. We had gone through so much since quitting our jobs four years earlier. I had wanted to quit, throw in the towel, run and hide, but we had other humans depending on us for security, for necessary survival needs, but mostly they were also witnessing how we walked the walk. We encouraged them in our journey that we can all do anything we want to in life.

If we would have waited until we were not scared anymore, we would still be working at FedEx and the high school. That single statement made me realize we would have to work hard and continue to sow day in and day out, and not get in a coasting and complacency mindset. I expected him to react like a proud papa to our end of year sales after we rallied and dominated into the top ten agents in our market center. I knew deep down he was proud, but there was a lesson he was teaching us that carried on with me to this day. I don't ever take our database, which is our tribe, for granted. Those are the people who like and trust us, who we have served at a high level, and who believe in us. They are the reason we get to do what we were born to do.

Jim took the time to write a strategic plan for us to become millionaires. I still have the paper and will cherish this relationship and his belief in us and our God-given potential. Today we are completely debt free and we are living the life we've always dreamed of living. This seemed like an impossible feat at one time. One of the reasons we were able to achieve this was by having coaches and mentors.

Ben Kinney was another relatable powerhouse leader who inspired us. He is a Keller Williams agent whose classes I was fortunate to attend. He taught me everything from getting clients to business planning and systems. Ben was a cable guy. He grew up in a one-room shack and was literally dirt poor. He loves to fish, hunt, and spend time with family and friends. He is one of us. When he bought his first apartment, the agent saw something in him and gifted him *The Millionaire Real Estate Agent*, a book by our founder, Gary Keller. Ben is now recognized as one of the most powerful, influential people in real estate. He is humble, and fiercely generous with his time, resources, and teachings. We were blessed enough to be directly taught the foundational ways to not only build a business but create a legacy to ultimately be able to give more. Ben Kinney Companies has started numerous companies in the real estate tech-space as well as coaching and training. Out of nowhere last year, one of his start-ups, Place, reached a value of $100 million in the Series A round, led by Goldman Sachs Asset Management, with a valuation of $1 Billion. I mention Ben in hopes that it anchors with you that if you set your mind to something, surround yourself with experts, mentors and coaches, and are willing to do the work, you can have no ceiling.

We were also coached by Vija Williams. She is one of the top luxury agents in the nation. She now serves as Director of Growth for the Ben Kinney Companies. She taught us so much and helped us expand our expectations and vision for our lives and dreams.

"When moving the needle forward, it's easy to get discouraged or overwhelmed. My success has come from staying focused on the process, not the outcome. Every day matters. Daily progress can feel incremental, but while the days are long, the years are short. I have found that when you are laser focused on the daily process, the score takes care of itself." -Vija Williams

I have always been so inspired by my own mentors and coaches that it is a natural progression for me to want to walk that path myself. I have received offers to coach for a couple of the best coaching companies in the nation now. Pinch me! I feel like there is just a genuine purity and reward in helping others create goals and take actionable steps that turn into more than dreams, but into a reality. The opportunity to help others build wealth, create financial freedom, and become who they were meant to be in answering their great calling in life is priceless. I heard a quote that someone said, "We teach who we are." That really spoke to me as we bring our own identity and experiences into how we share and teach.

Some people don't have the resources to hire a coach. Some will argue that you can't afford not to. But in the case that you don't have an in-person mentor or coach, no problem! The beauty of the internet is you can find teaching, coaching, tutorials, and testimonials on YouTube to watch at your convenience. I personally love podcasts. There are oodles of podcasts on any subject or topic you search for. The possibilities are endless when finding content to listen to. My recommendation is to be in a position where you can take notes. If you are listening to podcasts on the go in your car or during your workout, download the show notes so you can highlight and implement things that reverberate in you. I can tell you, I consider that I have about five mentors. Every week I am allowing them to pour into my life and I am implementing and taking actionable steps from their influence. I don't have to step foot out of my home. It is imperative you employ people in your life to hold you accountable.

One of my favorite stories is something that recently happened to me. I was listening to Grant Baldwin on a podcast about public speaking. I don't have a public speaking coach, but I am coached by Grant through his books and podcasts. Check out his resources if you are interested in public speaking. He is a great guy and brings it! He was interviewing a gentleman by the name of Jesse Cole. I will mention him often as he is literally my spirit animal. I felt like this guy was my brother from another mother. I immediately started googling him, his company, his new book, and his mission. I ordered his book and there was a delay in getting it, but when I did receive it, I dove in and was not disappointed. I reached out to Jesse through LinkedIn. I honestly could tell by his interview and book that he is a very approachable person. I strongly suspected he would personally reply back.

Jesse Cole

Owner of Savannah Bananas, Author of *Find Your Yellow Tux*, Keynote Speaker, Host of *Business Done Differently* Podcast

FEB 24

TROY AND DENISE SCHRODER sent the following message at 3:44 PM

I am reading your book now and I feel such a strong connection to your story. We have used out of the box marketing and innovation to sell 500 homes in seven years after someone told me twenty years ago that I could never stand out in a saturated industry! Serve/love people well and be distinctively different!

Jesse Cole sent the following message at 7:41 PM

Wow - love it and so great to hear! Thank you for sharing - Keep Standing Out!

It only took him just under four hours to respond. I was moved, not only by his book, but by his determination. His mission to do the opposite of normal resonated with me in a profound way. He is the Yellow Tux Guy. I do not wear a yellow tux, but I realized I had been doing business the way Jesse has, and I have never met anyone else I connected with in this way. I felt like I knew him because his writing style is very vulnerable, and I felt very connected.

There is a character max on LinkedIn messages, so I knew I wanted to share more. I emailed both him and his president, Jared Orton. I shared, well I overshared, our story and mission and how doing business differently is something we have wildly in common. I was BOLD and asked if I could be on their podcast! The old broken, insecure, defeated girl would NOT have ever put herself out there. That would have been way too vulnerable to being rejected. But here I am, new and improved! I was not sure I could even get a response. At this point in his career and celebrity status, I assume he gets inundated with fans reaching out. Their organization and its energy is truly contagious and recognized worldwide. However, I did get a response a few hours later telling me they loved our story and were happy to invite me as a guest on the podcast!

I can remember lying in bed and Troy saying, "You got an email about being invited to be on Bananas for Business."

I squealed and sprang out of bed to go investigate the email on my desktop and see it with my own eyes. And it was true, all because I asked. I know my greater calling is that we have a story to tell. My testimony is jam packed with defeats, failures, train wreck situations, hurt and a lot of rejection, which makes where we are today all the more relatable.

After we recorded the podcast, I got an email from Jared Orton, President of Savannah Bananas. He said he loved our conversation and was inspired and had already shared some ideas from our chat. Can you believe one of the most unique businesses in the country was taking note of some of our practices and ideas? I was on cloud nine, cloud 100 really. This was such a compliment coming from a person and an organization who has revolutionized the customer service experience. I will never forget how that one sentence he wrote made me feel. The best idea I had was shooting Jesse Cole a message telling him how inspired I am by his life, mission, and book.

Reaching out to authors can give you connections and opportunities you may not even realize are possible. I have no fear in putting myself out there anymore. I have gotten over being so scared of rejection. I am more frightened of my overwhelming feelings of regret if I don't take the shot. I had so much negative dialogue with myself over the two decades before I attained my real estate license. I was my own worst enemy back then. Now, the resounding voice in my head sounds just like Michael Jordan when he says, "I will miss one hundred percent of the shots I don't take." That keeps me going! I went a couple of decades sitting on the bench only daydreaming about the plays I would make. I dreamt about getting on the field, and even created plays and a plan in my head. Two decades LOST because I did not believe in myself enough. Two decades lost because I was pigeon-holed living others' plans and directives, while my main objective was pleasing others at the monumental loss of myself. Those days are in my rearview mirror.

What are you afraid of? What is holding you back? If the worst thing that happened was I never got a response or received a "no," it is okay. I know I am putting myself out there and I know I won't be granted every opportunity I apply for or seek. I sure as heck won't get any opportunities from the things I do not at least try for. I am going to worry less about the possible rejection and more about the possibility I can achieve more by risking my comfort zone. Conviction is not comfortable, I have learned. I am not going to allow myself to be a hostage to fear. Anytime I feel convicted to do anything big and new, fear may set in. In my experience, the most life changing things have happened on the other side of sheer terror. When I feel fear and start to adopt a scarcity mentality, I know there is a blessing on the other side if I just push myself and get out of my own way! When Troy and I quit our full-time jobs, newly married with five hungry, hormonal teenagers, it was paralyzing and frightening. It is also one of the biggest risks I have ever taken. To make matters more intense, all eyes were on us, on this radical decision we had made. I can remember breaking out in hives when I turned my resignation letter in to my boss. My palms were sweaty, and I felt like I was about to burst into tears. The moment I handed it to her, I started to pull the paper back. Then she pulled it back, not knowing what it was and probably wondering why I was seemingly playing a stupid game of tug-of-war. Handing in that letter was so spine-chilling. I was in essence saying farewell to a salary and benefits. But.what I was saying hello to was a limitless, ceiling-free, greater calling. I was saying yes to an opportunity to build an empire with the man of my dreams. I was finally going after the American Dream. When I switched gears in my brain, I was elated and grateful for the guts, the grit, and spring in my step to take the leap of faith and never look back.

It was our opportunity to show our kids, who were teens and old enough to be in tune with our every move, that you can do anything you put your mind to. The most colossal thing I wanted to instill in our kids through this process was to do whatever it takes and never give up. We were going to change the economy in our household of a limiting belief mindset. When we quit our jobs, remember the path. The path was not easy. We worked in three different sales industries before landing on the track to finally pursue real estate. We may have had bad days and wanted to quit, but we had too many dependents counting on us, not only to provide food and shelter, but to show them what we were made of!

Another way to connect with more successful people in your community is LinkedIn. Simply do a CEO search in your area. I send a short message (there is a character max) and let them know I would love to connect and have coffee. I found one woman who I had heard a lot of good things about and wanted to connect to see if we could reciprocate some business. I reached out, got a response, became Facebook friends, and she is now going to join a networking group for high income earning CEOs in our city. I wanted to create a safe place for a small, diversified group of women to collaborate, be one another's accountability partners, problem solve, and reciprocate. Oftentimes, the CEOs don't have a safe place to turn to mastermind with others. We can add value to each other and truly see things through a different perspective being in diverse industries. I have found that I honestly don't compare myself to other realtors in our community. We focus on how to be different, not replicating others. I often see people replicating our ideas. This is absolutely a compliment to us. My old mentality would have been very different, reacting that someone was stealing our ideas. Now I see that imitation is one of the finest forms of flattery.

Surround yourself with greatness.

Seek out people who are succeeding, not just in business, but in life. Any success in business will be affected negatively if your home life is a wreck. Success is orchestrating all the spokes, creating leverage, and implementing margin and balance in your life. I am a coach and mentor first and foremost to our children. Don't just talk the talk, walk the walk. We not only wanted to be intentional about seeking out "connecters" but wanted to reciprocate that for others in a big way.

The fact is, you don't grow when you are comfortable. We knew to get where we wanted to go, we needed to follow other successful agents who have gone before us. For us, it was joining a brokerage that was known for being the number one in training in any industry, not just real estate. Training, coaching, and mentorship were the cornerstone of building a sustainable business.

Do an audit of who is influencing and empowering your life!

Be around the light bringers,
the magic makers, the world shifters,
the game shakers.
They challenge you, break you open,
uplift and expand you.
They don't let you play small with your life.
These heartbeats are your people.
These people are your tribe.

DANIELLE ROBY QUOTE

Do you have a coach or mentor?

What steps do you need to take to make this happen?

What podcasts are you listening to?

What books are you reading?

Who are the leaders in your community you would like to connect with and learn to grow from?

Start pursuing others to be in community with who stretch you, hold you accountable, and teach you.

Chapter 5
Let the Courting Begin, Date your Database

One of the first things we learned from Cyndi Carfrey, our productivity coach when we started real estate, was to drill down and generate our database (aka goldmine)!

People underestimate the power of a database! People have the erroneous perception that a realtor gets their license, and the phone just immediately starts ringing. It would be a dream if we just hung our license with a broker of choice and became an order taker. Since this is not the case, valuable tools like a database are essential. The database is yours and it is free to create. It will prosper if you are consistently managing it well. The database is a propellant to your business. You own it so you must feed, water, nurture, and even prune and deadhead it!

One of the first and most important steps to being successful is creating your database. We all have a sphere of influence. We have family, friends, former or present schoolmates, co-workers, former co-workers. If you are new to a city, don't let this be a limitation. Yes, as a newcomer, you have to do more groundwork, but it will only make you appreciate the organic growth even more. You will have to be aggressive, relentless, and intentional about joining several networking groups. You also have to get comfortable asking others to help you make connections. Don't be fearful of inviting a network leader or highly influential person to coffee for a more intimate, deeper conversation than the typical speed dating vibe at networking events. Share your story, your grit, and your "why." I have found it so rewarding when people want my expertise, guidance, referrals, or references and I can go all in on what they stand for. Another aggressive way to build your database is to offer to host Open Houses for other realtors that have great listings. When you are marketing the Open House, you are putting your name out there to gain recognition.

Until you have your own listings to host, seek other high-producing agents who are grateful for competent, hungry new realtors like yourself. (More on the value of Open Houses in an upcoming chapter.)

When we first began, I sat down with my cell phone, and my Facebook friends list—a memory jogger for all the industries I do and have done business with. The mere thought of trying to edit the public perception of myself as the secretary and my husband as the handsome FedEx guy seemed daunting. We were going to be asking for others to hand their largest financial investment to us, with little to no experience, only a truckload of determination. I knew I wanted to be competent and provide the best service and results possible.

Troy and I sat down and jumped in headfirst with compiling our list. We had so many contacts at my very fingertips going back through several jobs in the past, tons of Facebook friends, etc. I was making separate lists to actually contact some of them the way I usually do. People I have more consistent contact with, those that I have a phone call, texting, frequent Facebook interactions, email relationship, etc. I would touch those contacts on a deeper, more personal level. For the others, I would draft my announcement letter. I told my story and conveyed how on fire we were to start this endeavor. My negative self-talk and fear was being *that person* who everyone blocked, snoozed, deleted, unfollowed, or just cringed when they saw my name. I am not a high pressure, magpie type salesperson. That is not who I am.

If you do not already have a single, streamlined way of organizing your real estate database and network, this should be next on your agenda. Many realtors and other business professionals rely on a CRM, or customer relationship management tool. There are so many great ones on the market and your market center may offer one within your company. It is imperative to have some kind of a system that helps you manage this element of your business. It is of the utmost importance.

Categorize, tag, and organize into groups how you know your contacts for an easy breakdown: friends, family, business owners, vendors. You will produce a buyer prospect and seller prospect list when you start to gain momentum and begin having these conversations about what their real estate related plans are for the year and how you can help! If they have a preferred real estate professional, do not be too shy to ask if you can continue to reach out and keep them on your list to be their plan B in case anything ever changes. Explain your motives are not to spam them in any way.

You will also need to send out a carefully constructed announcement letter. You cannot just post on Facebook and assume that all your friends and family saw your career change and new endeavor. Once you have sent out your announcement letter, you have to have a plan of how often and in which mode you will communicate with them. Keller Williams has a great training program, along with a productivity coach, which helped hold us accountable for adding our database to a 33-touch program.

Pretend you are dating your database. Well, that depends on your dating style. If you are a stage-four clinger/stalker type, nix that idea! My goal was to WOO. The definition of *woo* is to gain love; adoration; seek the favor of; support; or court. You don't want to smother your sphere, just drip love on them so they know you are there for any real estate needs their friends or family may have. The last thing you want is your clients feeling they need to file a VPO on you, or the social media equivalent, BLOCKING you! You must truly nurture your database, feed it, and respect it. Your database is your goldmine. Treat it as such or it can wither up and die. Don't take it for granted or yes, you will be shocked to learn that certain folks break up with you.

Today, with a database of over 2,000, it can be overwhelming. It is such a blessing and a great responsibility. You cannot neglect your crop at any stage, or it will not come to fruition and be as bountiful as it has the potential to be. Our database is like a newborn babe. It needs constant attention, and sadly it is something that gets overlooked or dismissed. Make this your priority in your business and you will see it grow, prosper and be rich in relationships.

We have had to reclassify our database and continue to tweak, scrub, evaluate, and break it down to our top fifty and top one hundred, and those we are making regular touches with and interactions with on social media, etc. So many of your past clients are not going to respond, engage, or come to client appreciation events, etc., but you still must keep in touch consistently. There is a staggering statistic that only about twenty-four percent of the consumers use the same agent that sold them their home when they move. Twenty-four percent? That statistic is absolutely unacceptable in my world. Not on my watch. We have to do a better job and continue the conversation and relationships past the transaction. This is true for any and every industry. The follow through with the relationship does not end once the client has purchased or sold. It is just the beginning. It is such a blessing and a great responsibility to nurture your past clients.

Some of our biggest cheerleaders and evangelists, as I call them, have never even bought or sold a home. They have lived in their homes for decades. They have seen consistent sold signs in neighborhoods or have witnessed how we serve and treat people, added us as friends on Facebook/Instagram and JUMP at the chance to refer us to anyone that even whispers a real estate need. Being a farmer's daughter, I truly understand the process of planting, nurturing, growing, and harvesting. You cannot neglect your crop at any stage, or it will not come to fruition and be as bountiful as it has the potential to be.

Your database is something that is not just on your to-do list daily. It should be at the TOP of your *opportunity* list! You will always be modifying it, adding to it, even subtracting from it when needed, and nurturing it constantly! It is not a one and done. I strongly urge you to take meticulous notes within your CRM or excel spreadsheet, including the names of spouses, children, even pets! Also, note their hobbies, favorite restaurants, etc. When we have a new client, you have them fill out a getting-to-know-you form. This is a fantastic and easy way to get your clients to tell you their favorite things, and you can reference those anytime in the future! You are not staying in touch to sell. You offer a great service. Unfortunately, there is only a small pool in every industry that exceeds expectations and truly extends an experience. Stay top of mind in relationships and reward those who refer you to new clients. This is the heartbeat of your business. The ultimate goal is to have other people marketing for you.

Here are some quick tips:

Google a mind jogger (there are many free lists online).

Download data from your social media accounts.

Whether you use Gmail, Yahoo, or Microsoft Outlook, you should be able to download your contacts.

Employ your close family to get additional addresses from their sphere of influence, if they are willing to share.

Whatever CRM you choose, you are not just collecting names, numbers, and addresses. You are in the business of relationships. Your notes should consist of their children's names, ages, pets if applicable, birthdays, hobbies, profession, their favorite things. When you are making calls, texts, emails, refer back to your notes to make it as intimate and personal as possible. I urge you to have at least 200 in your database out of the gate and continue daily to feed it and nurture it. Treat your database like a child. It has everyday needs to be met for it to continue to grow and flourish. If you give your database the daily attention it deserves, big things will happen, and you will see gigantic results. You will organically begin your strategic plan to network from interacting and engaging with your database.

Chapter 6
It is time to mingle!

When I was just starting out in life, I was in every show troupe, pop group, musical, show choir, soloist competition that was possible for me to be involved in. I remember auditioning my freshman year of college for The World Traveling Roustabouts. It was an elite show troupe that featured a costume change for every song, high level choreography and an opportunity to be a soloist and travel! There were forty-two females auditioning and two would make the cut. We had to perform two songs, sight read blindly in front of a panel, and then quickly learn a choreographed dance to perform immediately with little to no thought or preparation. I made it! I truly felt like a rock star. In my little bubble on the Northern Oklahoma college campus, I honestly felt like I was famous, even though I clearly was nowhere even remotely close. The opportunity paid for most of my college, and though it did not land me any record deals, the experience was priceless, and the friendships continued on. The point here is that I mingled, and it produced great results!

If you are socially awkward, remember, you only grow when you are uncomfortable. At times you hear this dirty word, and it induces you to feel like you need a barf bag! When you get close to your comfort zone, you will hear your border patrol screaming and setting off sirens. Be on the edge of your comfort zone. When you get close to your comfort zone boundary, your border patrol will scream at you. Don't be concerned when your border patrol is screaming at you. Be alarmed when you don't hear them warning you at all. However, if you are a social butterfly, this will be easy for you. Real estate is in fact a contact sport.

Seek to join your local chamber, networking groups, and your local homeowner's associations. If you don't own a home or live in a home that has a homeowner's association, you can still volunteer to start a

Facebook page or host a couple of neighborhood events a year to create a deeper connection among your neighbors while forming relationships that could in turn be future business. (We will discuss more in depth in a later chapter.) In my old neighborhood, I helped create our Facebook page and it was great having credibility and interaction with my neighbors that I may not have normally had. I was also able to write human interest stories and submit a picture of our neighborhood HOA meeting and have it published in the local paper. If you wish to truly come from a place of contribution, offer to host a Neighborhood Night Out snow cone or ice cream party. It is an opportunity for you to give a local business some massive exposure and provide a reasonable, fun activity. It is also yet another opportunity to get published in the local newspaper as well as your neighborhood newsletter. Who won't come out for free ice cream or a snow cone? You had me at the snow cone!

Networking Groups: There are many networking groups you can join. For example, your local chamber, Rotary, Lion's Club, Mom's clubs, Meetup.com, countless groups on Facebook and oodles more online. Your goal is to develop long-term, meaningful relationships with quality business professionals who are ready and willing to help you accomplish your business goals. You want to be their number one trusted real estate professional that is top of mind when anyone utters a real estate want or need within their earshot. Don't be discouraged if they already have a Plan A real estate professional. The stats are staggering regarding agents not being able to last for the long haul. Many will also move, retire, or simply not keep in touch. Be bold and ask to be their Plan B. Ask permission to stay in touch and you will be pleasantly surprised to move into the number one position as the trusted resource.

Another mentor, Mo Anderson, said her mother taught her from a young age to not only just get involved in organizations, but become a member of their boards and join committees. Don't just join and then sit on the sidelines like a couch potato. Find groups who stand for things you love, then show others you are passionate about the mission at hand and the relationships will come. When you are able to allow people to see the person you are behind your business card, you will receive more referrals than showboating your awards and expecting accolades. Be a giver and the blessings truly come back ten-fold.

You must get out from behind your desk! You can't hide or be a secret agent. People are your business! You need to be either serving, selling, or meeting new people. Love the people that have chosen you to be their go-to for any real estate need they or their friends or family anticipate. Don't go with someone to these events and curl up in the corner. If you want to play that role, you should just stay home and binge watch Netflix and eat bon-bons. Mingle and make a goal to not leave any one event without connecting and exchanging cards and data with at least three people! Remember, you are feeding your database to keep it alive!

If you can't find a group you feel connected to or drawn to or one that even exists, start your own. You are not going to get out of being involved in your communities if you want to grow your name branding, build credibility and reputation, and most importantly, forge relationships. I love the site Meetup. You can start a group there and develop a community or start a Facebook group and handpick people you think would be a great fit for your group. It does not have to be big to be effective. I have thrived and grown in small groups where the conversations are deeper and the atmosphere more intimate, where you can let your hair down and be more vulnerable, than spilling your business challenges in front of mere strangers.

Remember, joining your organizations or attending networking groups of any kind is not about card-giving. It is about card taking and collecting their data! I can detect a fake person that is not genuine a mile away. It is truly a gift of discernment. Make certain your intentions are pure or you may as well just stop, drop, and roll. Ultimately, it is about starting a bona fide relationship with them, not just having another person to add to your database. Plug them into your database, not to spam, but to keep in touch and adopt them to your sphere. Have the mentality to help others and seek out how to give more than expect what you can get. Follow up with a handwritten card and invite them to coffee if you want to visit more. There has to be an intentional follow-up system, whether it is through a robust CRM or simply calendar reminders, excel spreadsheets, or an old-fashioned notebook.

Whatever works for you, just hold yourself accountable. When I was a personal trainer, the clients loved to shift blame onto me if they had not lost weight that week. I can distinctly remember a lady named Susan coming to do her weigh-in. She literally had caramel from just taking a bite of a Snickers bar. The remaining candy bar was smashed in her back pocket. When she said my program just was not working, I was frustrated. I was not holding these clients at gunpoint to get in shape. They came to me and hired me as their expert. So you see, we can teach, train, and send others out to do the work, but it is up to us to hold ourselves accountable to do the actionable steps and understand every choice and decision dictates our outcome and future. Make the decision to lead yourself first and be committed to your accountability partners you have.

When you start out on this journey to become self-employed and be your own boss, there is a real paradigm shift. The mentality that we will get our real estate license, do a Facebook post, put a cheesy magnet on the side of our cars, and become an order taker is not reality.

The internet is a powerful tool, don't get me wrong. However, it will NEVER replace the kneecap-to-kneecap, belly-button-to-belly-button way of building trust and loyalty through relationships and people.

I am purposefully forming a tribe as we speak. I have been scouring a women's group to select high performing, successful women who are high level CEOs in other industries. My goal is to have 10-15 of us that meet on a regular basis. We have three now and the group is tight already. We have a safe environment where we can speak on not just highs and wins but challenges, failures, and struggles within our business. Collaboratively, we can come up with positive solutions, because sometimes when you are the one walking in the challenge you don't see the light. With so much careful thought, I have named this group Glow Givers. There are so many names of groups with powerful women, but I wanted a name that tells you this group will share and serve a purpose in building and helping one another. So many individuals that go to networking groups have one thing on their mind: "What is in it for me?" or "How many people can I literally speed talk to and give my elevator spiel to?" It has gotten to the point I have had people spitting in my face and getting in my personal space. This is not going to help you build relationships. This is what frankly prompts me to block your number or avoid eye contact when I see you at an event. No one wants to have a vulture or car salesman type chasing after them to see how you can serve them. These types of consumers are the last businesses I will refer my friends and family to. I have found when your intent and expectation is learning, serving, and helping others, the blessings show up ten-fold.

For our small group of rockstars, we agree on a podcast that interests all of us. We listen to a podcast a week and then go over our notes, thoughts, and ideas stemming from what we learned. It is so easy to listen to a podcast even when you are on the go. When we get together twice monthly, it is for about an hour and a half. Our goal is to edify, amplify, empower, and hold one another accountable. We truly give permission for each other to pour into our lives in a transparent, honest way. We leave knowing that we have helped recharge one another and relight the fires in our bellies that sometimes need a powerful ignition.

I am a sap for a love story! My mom helped plan weddings at our local church. She was the jack of all trades. She could decorate, design the flower arrangements, bake the wedding cake and make the mints, and help give the bride a once-in-a-lifetime day. I have a love for weddings that runs deep. I have probably watched every Lifetime movie known to man. Establish a relationship with local wedding planners. You can offer to donate a package in their presentation packet about buying a home. You can also set up at wedding expos and offer an attractive drawing to collect data and hopefully pick up some love smitten new clients. Trust me, there is nothing more fun and rewarding than house hunting with newlyweds! Cue the video of him carrying her over the threshold. Love it!

If you want to start a hobby club, this is an organic, fun way to meet others with common interests. Are you a gardener, a great cook, a cyclist, runner, power walker, photographer? You can create a group by invite only if you would like to keep it smaller and more intimate or allow anyone to invite people. When you mutually love doing something, relationships blossom so naturally. You don't have to come across with a vulture sales vibe. As you get to know one another in the group, your profession can come up, you don't have to lead with it. You can also start small. Don't get bogged down with thinking you need to create a community of fifty to one hundred people to mark it as a success. The whole purpose is to build quality and loyal relationships that have sustainability. Quality above quantity wins!

I started a cooking demo class! What a hit! It is like Denise Schroder's bad cooking lessons mixed with a *Fear Factor* vibe. Below we are trying spicy chicken feet! Talk about stepping out of our comfort zones. It seemed more like an episode of *Fear Factor*, but we had so many laughs!

SMILING ON THE OUTSIDE WHILE EACH OF US
LITERALLY THREW UP IN OUR MOUTHS.

I am also teaming up on Facebook live and/or Instagram live with great cooks all over the country. One of the contestants from a prior season of *Worst Cooks in America*, Frank Scuderi (aka Frankie Meatball), taught me how to make homemade meatballs! I am going to teach him how to make a famous Oklahoma side dish. We will have fun and it will be comedic content for both of our social media platforms. It all depends on your personality and how you run your social media if this kind of thing is a fit for you. You can simply orchestrate a walking club by hopping on your neighborhood Facebook page, for example. Do not underestimate the power of just putting yourself out there and meeting new people. Please note, I am just learning to cook so I am nowhere near an expert, but I am willing to show up, be vulnerable, self-deprecating, and learn new things with an audience. Recently, I have started teaching our new grandbaby how to cook. Lord, help him! I am teaching him very young how to use a fire extinguisher and burn stuff!

Our past client and someone I call friend called me this past week. Alyssa has started a baking company. We masterminded on the phone, and I was able to give her a few unique ideas to pursue to get new business and momentum. One simple idea was to offer to host a kid's birthday party. Alyssa will provide the mini cakes, icing, decorative tools, and setup, etc. She can teach them how to decorate their own cake. The video content will be so cute, organic, and comical! What a great Facebook life (be sure to also get media releases signed when you use anyone in your social media, etc.). I also offered for her to come over to my kitchen and do a demonstration of herself decorating a cake and also teaching me to do one alongside her. I can help her tap into my sphere of influence. When extending honest, genuine value to help others grow, blessings will overflow!

I have recently started doing some abstract painting and refurbishing all kinds of items that I thrift-flip. This is a process where I go to various thrift stores and pick up items I want to refurbish. I am doing video tutorials, reels, stories, and posts about my transformation of the projects. I have always been frugal, so my "Denise Designs on a Dime" posts get a lot of traction and engagement. This is a great way to connect, inspire, and entertain on social media platforms. We do our best to be very well-rounded on our social media presence. I want them to truly feel they know me and are doing life alongside us.

SHARE YOUR GIFTS, TALENTS AND HOBBY AND BUILD A FRESH, NEW COMMUNITY.

Do you have a hobby or something you are an expert in where you can get vulnerable and share? I am interested in design, crafting, and attempting to cook (very self-deprecating). One of my favorite things I do with thrift finds is find designer dupes and do a side by side of an item from a high-end store next to my edited transformation. Your passion does not have to directly relate to your profession. The goal of social media engagement is for your followers/sphere of influence, past clients, etc., to come to know you as a person. We consider this a networking spoke as well. I meet people who comment on my posts, and it creates a bond, giving us something in common. I have people now tagging me in all kinds of DIY craft, interior design type projects. They begin to think of me at the forefront of their mind, not only about real estate, but about cooking, painting, refurbishing thrift items, fashion, crafting, and interior design. To get your audience involved, ask them for their favorite DIY's or suggestions on how you could improve your skills. I receive great responses and active engagement. You also find new folks online you can build rapport with and form a deeper connection based on something you found you have in common.

You can recruit a friend or family member to run your video camera or invest in a reasonable tripod that is compatible for cell phones. For $20, you have a set-up in good lighting to jump in with both feet and do some videos!

Another fun idea I have is a wine club! We had a blast sponsoring a local wine club event a couple of years ago. We just bought a used boat and I want to invite an intimate group, two a month, to go out on the boat. We will try a new kind of wine and do some fishing at sunset. It is just a couple of hours but serves as offering something different for our clients/friends. I want to call this exclusive invitation Fishin' n Sippin'!

I am also going to have a Vision Board Party now yearly. I am so very passionate about this! Troy and I made vision boards when we first started real estate. Like the Bible says, where there is no vision, the people will perish. We have had so much fun looking back at our vision board and seeing all the dreams that have fully come to fruition. We need to update our boards, so I want to share this experience with others.

Another clever way to connect with people at major local events is the check-in feature on Facebook. You can check to see which of your friends are physically nearby. For example, we went to the state fair here in Oklahoma City. We posted on our wall, "CHECK IN, WHO ELSE IS HERE, LET'S MEET UP!" We got many responses and we messaged those that were "checked in" at the fair. We stayed in one spot and encouraged people to come say hi. We were able to visit with several friends and clients by being intentional. You can take this approach at football games, carnivals, movies in the park, or really any local event where a lot of people will gather. It is hard to keep up and stay in touch with so many. This is a fun, spontaneous way to reach out and say hello or catch up when you are in mutual locations with your clients you may not ever run into otherwise.

It is not who we know, but who KNOWS us!!!

When someone so much as whispers the word real estate, who will share your name as the number one, go-to real estate professional?

When we think about networking, we need to change our mindset. Go into these groups looking for ways to seek to understand everyone else's business. I have had the most gratifying experiences with people when my intentions are to help grow their business or organization. I am expecting nothing in return. The law of reciprocity is so powerful. When you help others, they will then yearn to help you in return. When you are extending a hand to others, it will come back tenfold. Our motto with networking has become more unconventional. Of course, during Covid, these networking meetings ceased. We have to constantly pivot and get in step with the times in order to not fall behind.

Chapter 7
Open Houses

A funny story my mom used to tell was that I broke her water and came out of the womb with high heels on. Since I was able to talk, I was a performer. You could never take a candid photo of me. I have some sixth sense when there are any cameras on me, telling me to strike the perfect pose. I did the duck face pose before it was even cool! One story that depicts my personality is the time when I was only three years old, standing up on a stool in my pink leotard and tights. I was singing, dancing, begging, well, rather demanding that my younger cousins be still and quiet because it was "my show." In this same way, the Open House is your show!

Open Houses can be extremely effective. Time being your main investment, it is great for any budget. If you are going to host an Open House, ramp it up! Make a valiant, concerted effort to pack the house! Treat your Open House preparation as you would for a special party at your home. Every detail and box you check truly counts. Convey to your sellers that bringing in traffic is your top priority.

*What can you do to stand out?

*What can you implement TODAY that no one else is doing?

Being different does not have to cost more money out of your marketing budget. You can use tactics that you have to invest a little in, but spending money is not necessary. Get your creative juices flowing.

Some sellers do not care to do an Open House with the new digital age. Their house is on display twenty-four hours a day. With the new 3D video tours, people can really get a feel for the property, it is amazing. We have had sellers think unqualified buyers may be casing their homes. Make sure to go over all the information with the sellers and address the pros/cons, then let them ultimately decide if they wish for you to host one on their behalf.

There are some agents that do not care for them and do not implement them into their marketing plan whatsoever. This is up to you in how you create your business plan for lead generating. To state the obvious, every client and case is different, so assess it accordingly.

Open Houses are an incredible way for you as an agent to meet new people to add to your database and establish yourself as the neighborhood expert. Think about it, you market, and people come to you. It is a gift and opportunity to connect with many people at a time. Troy and I have never cold-called anyone in this business, such as expired listings or for sale by owner listings. We have focused on our database and sphere of influence and acted to identify true prospects around our open houses and listings.

First and foremost, what you put into it determines what you can expect it to yield. Market your Open House aggressively or you will likely just be sitting in an empty house, alone. You want all your efforts to be fruitful! Have a systemized, intentional plan of action. Here are some of the steps we follow in our perfect recipe for a successful Open House:

We put out signs on Monday and more directionals right before the Open House. When you post your signs for the Open House, do some quick videos. Video the neighborhood sign and discuss some great features and benefits about the subdivision. You can also talk about nearby restaurants, retail, schools, etc. Set the stage to pack your Open House. Another idea is to ask some of the local businesses to provide a code or coupon you can hand out to the guests. People love free stuff and coupons. This is also a networking effort, setting the tone for building reciprocal relationships with businesses in the areas you home in on and farm.

We enter it in the MLS so that it syndicates out on the web.

We pay to boost posts on our business pages on FB/Instagram.

We post it to our stories on Twitter, LinkedIn, and send an email blast to our database.

We also post it in our local marketplace on Facebook. This gets the Open House even more exposure.

Ask your client to SHARE the Open House marketing post on their page and ASK all their friends and family to post. Just by asking people to SHARE in the text of the post, you will increase exposure exponentially. Explain you will multiply exposure to their friends and family by sharing.

First and foremost, give yourself plenty of time to prepare the home. It is a price war and a beauty contest! Shine sells and so does a good smelling home! Oftentimes, you will need to turn all the lights on, open the blinds to a desirable position, bring in your fresh flowers, spray air freshener throughout the house, play calming music from your phone or a television. Bring shoe covers/booties to protect your client's floors. We have had to quickly scrub toilets, wash windows, scoop poop in the backyard, and even clean a litter box. A great investment is an automatic bootie machine for your elderly guests. Please do not roll in the driveway to your Open House a couple of minutes before it starts. It looks so unprofessional for a consumer to be there waiting for you and the house is all dark. This is a show, the listing is the star. Preparation is key to present your client's biggest investment in the positive light needed to get it sold. Tape balloons to the mailbox and place multiple Open House signs all over the yard. Do what everyone else is NOT doing! The extra touches and efforts go a long way for your sellers and anyone driving by and coming to the Open House.

When you get to the Open House, make sure you do a Facebook Live/Instagram Live/YouTube Live video before arrivals. Show the public around the house and encourage people to come see you in the next couple of hours. If you have brought any giveaways or treats, draw your viewers in to come see a cute place and grab a goodie! Focus on the top amenities of the home to highlight. Make sure to not show the entire house, leave some mystery they must come see, some amazing feature you don't show. We have had friends, neighbors, past clients show up to see a beautiful home and it opens up opportunities for real estate conversations where you uncover a need they may have. It also will keep us top of mind as being top listing agents that are dominating an area. When people are ready to buy or sell, you are going to be their go-to!

Marketing on steroids is doing whatever it takes to stop traffic. You think stopping the scroll is hard? Try stopping actual traffic! I had so much fun doing this I was considering applying to be a human advertiser! Troy was hosting the Open House, while I was doing my best to draw people in from the neighborhood. This Open House had over fifty people come through it. In the winter and in our local area, this is an insane turnout.

MY GOAL HERE WAS TO STOP TRAFFIC AND PACK MY OPEN HOUSE. MISSION ACCOMPLISHED!

How about rolling out the red carpet at your Open House? Talk about a conversation starter that breaks the ice! It is a fun way to strike up a non-threatening chat right when they walk in the door. We offer a branded trinket and water bottles and sometimes cookies. (If you want to offer snacks, run this by your seller to assure it is okay.) Make people feel welcome and at home and then let them look. We do not stalk people or freak out if they do not wish to sign our guestbook. We always mention our MLS sheet has our contact information on it if they have any questions. Another strategy is not having any property flyers with you and asking for their email where you can send all the information pertaining to the house.

PEOPLE STROLL THROUGH OPEN HOUSES ALL THE TIME, GIVE THEM SOMETHING TO REMEMBER. MAKE IT AN EXPERIENCE THEY WON'T FORGET.

If you project vulture vibes when you ask guests to sign in, they will probably write their name down as Elvis or Mickey Mouse. Just be natural and non-threatening. You can have a sign-in at the door that states guests will be asked to sign in to protect the security of the seller. When you have an honest mindset that sees your offer of services as saving the patron from a bad realtor, your perspective shifts. You can alter your thinking that you are truly offering a service, not selling.

Another tip you can try is sprinkling your branded flyers and business cards all over the house. Some people are so scared to be sold to that they won't sign or even accept a flyer. They will, on the other hand, grab one at their leisure when they are placed throughout the house.

Our team focuses more on connecting with the patrons, building trust and rapport as quickly as we can, without being pushy. If you capture one viable client that results in a closing from each Open House, that is a success. Don't chase the wind trying to sell to everyone that walks in the door. Focus on conversation and genuine connection. Also, love the one you are with. If you are deep into conversation and really building some trust and rapport, don't abandon them to run after a new guest. However, NEVER ignore anyone! We have had a preferred lender come to host Open Houses with us. Your lender is a great resource to take over the conversation portion of the mortgage and pre-approval process. Utilize them as an extra person to help field your traffic and never waste an opportunity to personally interact. The lender can also be an extra person in the house for safety and help you to greet everyone. If you expect this is going to be a hot property with a record turnout, pay a newer agent to help you greet and direct traffic. You can't be everything to everyone.

Politely give each guest a flyer and then circle back around to further engage with them when they leave. It can be a juggling act handling multiple groups gracefully when you have people that are very engaged and potential customers. Don't give off that vibe like a creepy car salesman with hair that looks like he washed it with a pork chop. Just be natural and non-threatening. When people enter the Open House, greet them at the door, introduce yourself, shake their hand and jot their name down. We always point out the focal points and awesome features and amenities of the home and then tell them to make themselves at home. PLEASE don't ever be sitting and not showing the courtesy of welcoming them into the home. It gives off the impression they are a bother, when in fact, they are the reason you are hosting to begin with. I have attended so many Open Houses where the agent never left her chair and was on her phone playing solitaire without a care in the world. If you're going to be lazy and not care, then it's not worth the trouble of your seller's preparations for the event. Have a high energy and deep engagement; show that you are excited to be there and help them fall in love with the home. I also always have a notebook where I write any information they share; kid's names, pets, where they live now, occupations mentioned in conversation. I do NOT use my phone, because it sends a negative impression that I may be scrolling my social media accounts. When I am writing on a notepad it seems like I am more engaged in my Open House.

We always offer anyone who seems interested in the house the HOA covenants, floor plans, and a CMA on their own home, then pursue getting an appointment. Start off any conversation or relationship adding value before you ask for something. Give before you take!

If you snub your nose at nosey neighbors, don't! They are your 4-1-1 for the neighborhood and they could potentially be future sellers. Approximately twenty-six percent of neighbors know someone that is interested in the subdivision. The nosey neighbors are walking billboards to market your listing. Odds are, they love their neighborhood and would love to pick their neighbors.

We send the guests out the door with a branded item. It may be an ink pen, a notepad, a sports magnet, or a branded water bottle. For those attendees that shared their information and do not have a realtor, we send a quick video of the property again so they can have it for reference. In the video we simply express how nice it was to meet them and we are here if they need anything further. That is followed up by a handwritten card in the mailbox the very next morning with the same message and a business card. We are not spamming or stalking these folks. We are just adhering to a strict, systemized follow-up to give us a better shot at a future conversation or relationship. You can also share the KW app with them after you have explained how it benefits them in their house hunting efforts. You can educate them about how all the third-party hub sites are not connected to the MLS and may lead buyers on a rabbit chase. We had a client just yesterday inquire about two properties to view. After researching them, we found that one sold thirteen years ago and the other sold three years ago.

We recently just got hired due to these efforts after an Open House. We added them to our monthly mailout and newsletter list and sent a handwritten card that next day. They were a couple I knew from working together at my previous job years ago. After we had sold their home in a day and helped them purchase, the client did a testimonial video for us. He stated in the video that one of the reasons they chose us was the sentiment of the handwritten card. He mentioned they toured many Open Houses and met several realtors. We were the only ones who took the time to send a card directly after the Open House. This works, folks! This resulted in two sales!

You may be saying to yourself, "This all sounds great, but I have no listings." The beauty of hosting Open Houses is there are always agents that will allow you to host their listings. Keep in mind, it is a huge responsibility for an agent to allow you to hold their listing's Open. We are inviting you (the agent) to be an extension on our team in marketing and holding this property Open, so we have strict stipulations when other agents hold our listing's Open.

*Commit to posting signs.

*Be a student of this listing! Know the property details, features, and benefits inside and out. You are the expert, and you should always show up fully prepared.

*Research the neighborhood comps so you can be educated on the pulse of the market in case inquiring minds want to know more about the area.

*Provide prompt feedback within an agreed upon, reasonable time to the listing agent. The sellers are ALWAYS eager to find out what the feedback is on their home! It is nice if you can scan the portion of your forms with the feedback reflected.

We have had agents NOT post signs in advance, then show up late, not provide feedback, and act unprofessional with the attendees. We got a call on a $450,000 listing that the sellers wanted to release their realtors. It was a realtor we know and respect, so we asked more questions. The sellers expressed they were still doing last minute preparations for the Open House when the hosting agent showed up only a minute before the Open House. She did not post directional signs as she had committed to and admittedly knew nothing about the property. The sellers were very upset. They had hired a house cleaner to deep clean this 4,000-square-foot home and make sure the house was perfect. They held up their end of the deal, preparing their lawn, pool, and house. This agent acted like hosting was just really of no priority to her. Most of the time, the home is the seller's largest investment. We need to handle it with the utmost care and consideration. Hosting an Open House is not just warming a seat and directing traffic through a house. Our industry can get a bad rap for agents that act negligently and don't lead with integrity. The sellers wanted to hire us because they could tell we really care.

You can also buy neighborhood lists like Cole's directory to set up a Slydial call. Slydial is the cat's meow. It routes directly to the recipient's voicemail. You can announce the new listing and invite them, and also mention to look for an informational flyer on their door, etc. Not many agents do this, either. All of these steps are not only going to bring more people to view the house, but will show them your work ethic and what kind of aggressive service and exposure they would receive with a "Schroder Listing."

The day of the Open House, we post around ten directional signs, depending on the logistics. We arrive at the house about 12:30 for a 2:00 p.m. event. We walk to at least ten doors near the house and invite them to the Open House. We ask people to give us their opinion on the place, see if they want to pick their neighbors, and share why they LOVE the neighborhood. Finally, we do a live teaser video at the house to entice the general public to get off their duffs and tour the house!

For a more intimate event, do an exclusive Open House for the neighbors only. My favorite and best turnout has been when we do a

Twilight Toast. We provide wine, crackers, grapes, and a chill atmosphere. We post on the neighborhood Facebook page, if they have one. If you do not have privileges to post on it, ask your seller to post it for you. Post a sign in the yard that says, "SNEAK PEEK Exclusive Open House Invite Only." You can walk the neighborhood and post door hanger invites or tape a flyer on the door. This is a fantastic way to meet the neighbors and encourage them to come hang with their neighbors, tour a home, and have Happy Hour! I love doing these on Thursday nights. You can also use EZ Text and Slydial to send out reminders. There is a cost in this to purchase the phone lists and pay for the mass text and Slydial calls, but it is very reasonable and well worth it. You could send a paper invitation to the whole subdivision as well, if time and budget allows. To keep costs down, canvassing the neighborhood gives you a lot more opportunity to meet the neighbors and extend a personal invitation. Again, how many agents are canvassing neighborhoods to hand deliver invitations? The neighbors will see your initiative and work ethic as a rare one in this industry.

How many other homes are listed in the neighborhood? Collaborate with other agents to bring mass exposure to the Open Houses. There is power in numbers. It is a win/win for all involved. You could be as elaborate as a block party situation where you each offer something in the driveway. You could do lemonade, branded balloons, a hotdog, or cookies. It does not have to be outlandishly expensive. It will draw attention to your marketing efforts when you co-market with the other agents and gain traction for being different. It is a great way to meet neighbors as well.

Have you ever been showing a house or had an Open House, and the kids are going nuts? The children are running around like they have overdosed on sugar and adrenaline. Give them something to search for (something easy to find, not deep in the seller's cabinets or drawers, etc.), and offer a small prize if they find the item, a scavenger hunt vibe, if you will.

We had a gentleman come into one of our luxury Open Houses one time. He was very engaging. If you judge a book by its cover, you will get burned. This man was dressed like a homeless person and was driving a beater car. He began to share that he had been through three other Open Houses that very afternoon. Not one person spoke to him or gave him direct eye contact. No one even asked him to sign the guestbook. Their assumption was he could not afford these homes so why bother. He was left feeling hurt and invisible. It turned out that he was a cash buyer looking to spend up to $600,000. Treat everyone the same, no matter their appearance. It was heartbreaking to hear his account of how people made him feel like an outcast. Every single person that comes through the door should be greeted the same, with a smile and a warm handshake or fist bump! Remember the famous line in Pretty Woman when Julia Roberts walks into the luxury clothing store on Rodeo Drive and the sales associate treats her like she is trash. BIG MISTAKE!

Measure your results! For example, one year we served 104 families, 85 were referrals— repeat clients or others from our sphere of influence, the other eleven were Open Houses. Our average commission that year was $6,600 with an average home price of $220,000. That is $72,600 in G.C.I. WOW! This is no joke! Troy and I made about $70,000 combined in our former jobs! Don't minimize the life changing results Open Houses can offer. This is a great spoke to your lead generating plan. If you do one Open House a week, and even if you take four weeks off a year, focus on picking up one viable client that you get to the closing table. If one sale came to fruition from each of the forty-eight Open Houses you host, the results would be astounding! Drumroll please! That is $316,800 in G.C.I. Open Houses take time and energy, but not a lot of cost investment is incurred. I live in one of the cheapest places in the country to live. You may have a much higher average price point. If you choose to concentrate on Open Houses as one of your focus areas for lead generation, you can yield high profitability. The key is having a consistent, purposeful systemization in place. It is like a rinse and repeat. You do the same thing every time, it is just with a different property.

We built our business from our sphere of influence, tailoring a stellar customer service experience and Open Houses. Buying leads for cold calls can be costly and it is much harder to gain trust without meeting someone face to face. If you are going to have your seller go to all the trouble to prepare their largest asset, commit to knocking it out of the park with all your efforts to pack the Open House and generate a sale!

Between hosting Open Houses and preparing sellers to stage for showings, our team has learned all of the DO'S and DON'TS of what a home should look like when potential buyers walk through. To help, we've compiled our best tips for those who are putting their home on the market. When you live in a place long enough, it's easy to ignore the clutter or forget that some people may be turned off by seeing a litter box in the basement. This is a great checklist to run through before showings.

Remember: You only get one chance at a first impression.

Make it count!

Secure valuables (tech devices such as laptops, tablets, phones), bills (some have account numbers), spare keys to the house, and prescription drugs. Our favorite saying is, "Don't have any drugs, diamonds, or guns in the house."

Have all counter tops cleaned off. Remove countertop appliances such as toasters or coffee makers.

Keys and personal items should be stored away.

Declutter / put away everyday items: dishes, mail, shoes, coats, kids' toys, sporting equipment, etc.

Take fifteen minutes and organize / purge your fridge - because a buyer WILL look!

Make sure the thermostat is set appropriately for the weather and make the home comfortable for showings.

Take the trash out and consider hiding garbage cans.

Minimize family photos.

Do a thorough cleaning - even if you have to hire a cleaning service. It is a price war and a beauty contest.

Improve curb appeal: Mow the lawn and trim back overgrown shrubbery, mulch, paint shutters, weed gardens, address the trim, fix walkways, clean exterior windows, power wash home.

Make the bathrooms shine: Toilet seats down, clean mirrors and other glass surfaces.

Bake something that smells good. Chocolate chip cookies, apple pie. I've used the pre-made cookie dough and frozen pies for this. A pan of apple juice with cinnamon and cloves simmering in the oven works well and is easy.

Put fresh flowers or flowering plants on the dining room table.

Play soft music.

Turn on all of the lights.

Offer snacks and water.

Take all the magnets and pictures off the refrigerator.

If guns are in the house, make sure they are secured.

Open the windows - buyers love lots of natural light.

Stick all personal toiletries in a drawer or a basket. (No one wants to see your toothpaste or hand lotion).

Organize toys or store them while your home is on the market.

Less is more. Remove excess furniture if possible.

Replace light bulbs that are burnt out. The better the lighting, the better the results.

Walkways to and from the home should be clean and clear.

Hide feeding bowls, litter boxes, dog beds, etc. Some home-seekers have allergies and can be put-off by their presence.

Chapter 8
Knock, Knock.

When I was going through training at Keller Williams, I hated the thought of having to cold call or door knock. I thought to myself if this is how I had to do business, was it my cue to run to the nearest exit? I did not get into real estate to go spontaneously pop by someone's home who does not want to be sold to. Just the mere thought of door knocking made me physically ill. We had recently been doing door-to-door roof sales and it just was not my cup of tea. I hated this feeling, and it limited my belief in my purpose. I had to have a lot of conversations with myself about the positives of this activity outweighing my ridiculous objections. You can be fined in some neighborhoods so please find what you are allowed to do in case you need a permit to door knock. Neighborhood Watch folks will turn you in lickety-split if you are not following rules. There is a Mrs. Kravitz in every neighborhood. We used to have a neighbor that attempted to make citizen's arrests for people not wearing a bike helmet, so keep in mind to check your city/neighborhood ordinances about solicitation.

One of our action plans from day one was to prospect around our Open Houses. This is in conjunction with sending out our consistently branded Just Listed postcards. We would go door to door and hand out flyers and personally extend an invitation. When we go to the door, we are not trying to give a sales spiel, we are only offering an invite and encouraging them to swing by. Our script entails having a genuine conversation, that we love hearing from neighbors about what they love about their neighborhood and encouraging them to pick their neighbors. They can be genuinely curious about the value of their homes in their neighborhood. You can have some market analysis reports with you so you can offer them if someone requests one. We have been invited into homes to give tips and advice on updates, etc. We ended up listing a home for an elderly lady and helping her purchase through door knocking. I followed up with a handwritten card and some blueberry muffins. She was a widow and so grateful for the personal attention. When we were in her home, she had a realtor's information on her fridge. That made it all the sweeter that we were chosen to serve her. All these neighbors are potential sellers, so just enjoy getting to know them and present yourself as the neighborhood expert! Then add them to your campaign of potential sellers, dripping real love on them in the meantime.

We took door knocking to another level. We went to the NBA star Kevin Durant's door and left him a branded sports magnet and our business card. We confirmed it was his home because there were FedEx packages on his front porch addressed to him. I know you are thinking the ending to this story is he hired us to list his home when he moved to transfer to the Warriors. But he did not, we never heard from him. My son helped his grandfather coach at the same gym the OKC Thunder practiced at daily. He ran into Kevin one day and asked him if he got the magnet his mom left. I love my son's soft way of trying to get his mom exposure!

When you get a new listing, hosting an Open House is a great time to knock on as many doors as you can to maximize attendance and exposure. When you NEED a listing in a specific neighborhood, that is the perfect time to beat the streets. We also will send out a mailer to the entire area our clients are searching in if there is no inventory on the MLS and no knowledge that listings are coming up soon. Your postcard is a marquis. Use it to spell out loud and proud that "We have BUYERS who are dreaming about living in your neighborhood!" Door knocking these magnet neighborhoods shows a determination to work for your clients. It is bound to catch the attention of homeowners who don't normally see realtors hitting the streets searching for that needle in a haystack for their customer. As noted earlier, please follow your city guidelines if you need a permit to canvas a subdivision. The fines can be steep so do your homework before doing the heel-toe express. We have never had an issue handing out Open House or new listing flyers or taping them to a door with scotch tape. It can be such a fruitful way to stand out and give a taste of your tenacity in how you serve.

Chapter 9
Being different is your Superpower!

Not to sound like I am quoting famous lyrics from a Journey song, but I was just a small-town girl, a farmer's daughter with high hopes to someday move to the big city and make things happen. That was me. I am a performer, singer, creator, an artist, photographer, fashionista, interior designer in my own right, lover of people, high-heels, foodie, and food critic that can't cook... and one of the most tenacious and driven people you will ever know. I have always been known for loving big, laughing hard, and dreaming even bigger. One of my most proud attributes is distinctively, unapologetically being different.

Don't ever let the noise of others spewing negative chatter about you being silly or ridiculous take hold in your heart. I have struggled with being different my entire life. I have always colored outside the lines, gone against the grain, and been unattracted to the norm. I was strongly influenced by my family to be me. Being the black sheep in my family gave me training to have more confidence to be authentically me. Growing up, I was awkward. I was tall and lanky. I would often get teased and be called Olive Oil. I was very insecure until I was about a sophomore in high school. I then started gaining confidence. One way I always expressed myself was through my fashion and clothes. I love extra frills, flare, ruffles, lace, and literally anything edgy that gives my outfit the extra oomph!

I heard a saying that resonated with me. "You will be too much for some people, those are not your people." This saying speaks to me in so many ways. I have always been the girl that wants to make everyone laugh, and that may mean writing an original crazy song, doing a dance, or changing my tone of voice. Learn to embrace your quirky, unique side. Weird is good. Don't be afraid of being different, be more fearful of trying to be just like everyone else. Going through so many rejections and abandonments led me to feel I had to seek the approval of others around me. Some of that truly stems from a childhood feeling unloved and unworthy to be accepted by a natural parent. It took years of rewiring and working through things to come to the realization that I should choose people who choose me. I have this quote hanging up in my house so I will never forget it. Today, I am unapologetic in being me. I am uniquely and wonderfully made. I am proud of that and as an adult I see I inspire others. I have been able to help people think and creatively express themselves in a way they did not know was possible. Instead of asking permission from others to allow me to be me, I gave notice.

Don't focus on replicating exactly what your competition is doing.

Who are YOU? What makes you, YOU?

Do you think any of us will be remembered if we all look and act the same?

I was in a class taught by Mo Anderson, regional vice chairman of Keller Williams International. Mo has become such an impactful inspiration, mentor, and leader in our lives. She has many attributes that remind me of my own mother. I have always felt such a natural, organic connection with her since I met her. She created the culture within Keller Williams that drew us there and has kept us there. She authentically walks the walk of living life beautifully, both personally and professionally. Her accomplishments are mind boggling. At the spry age of eighty-five years young, she still wakes up every day with her purpose to make a difference in the lives of others and her community. Mo's recently published book, *A Joy-Filled Life: Lessons from a Tenant Farmer's Daughter...Who Became a CEO*, chronicles a truly American success story while encouraging readers to follow their own dreams, set high standards, and at all times, "do the right thing."

My favorite quote from Mo is, "When you face tough times but keep on going; when you're discouraged and doubtful, but still show up; when you are not sure of what to do, but you give it your best anyway--you will, in the end, succeed. Just be willing to do whatever it takes."

I hear her voice in my head saying, "Just do what it takes!" It is quite motivating, to say the least. She teaches an intense, beautiful class, Quantum Leap, based on personal and spiritual growth. The material does not leave room for sugar coating and tiptoeing around the truth. It is a class that forces you to take a deep, close-up look at your soul and prioritize what is really important at the end of the day. The class slows you down and taps into your emotional side in a deep, peeling layer kind of process.

MO ANDERSON, KELLER WILLIAMS INTERNATIONAL
REGIONAL VICE CHAIRMAN AND I

She showed us a video of Pike Place Fish Market in Seattle. I was utterly mesmerized with the business model of this company. Fish stink, they are slimy and quite ugly when they are lying dead with those bug eyes staring back at you through the glass. There is nothing sexy about a stinky fish, can we agree? It is cold, smelly, and highly laborious work. With that being said, I would go to work for this organization just to be a part of the phenomenon that they have created. This owner and staff have made their philosophy all about drawing people in.

Founded in 1930, the Pike Place Fish Market is an enduring Seattle institution. It became an internationally recognized business when in 1986, longtime owner, John Yokoyama, and his crew took a stand to become world famous. One of the fishmongers suggested the goal to become world famous and it developed into a clear vision. Up until that point, John had exhibited more of a tyrant management style. He changed his mindset and model to providing an interactive comedy show that you could be cast for by being a customer or simply walking by. You may get a fish thrown at you, so if you walk by the market, have your catching glove ready. You will see fish fly, orders echo, and infectious smiles and laughter like you have never experienced.

FLYING FISH AT PIKES PLACE MARKET

PIKES PLACE MARKET

In their book, *Fish: A Proven Way to Boost Morale and Improve Results,* authors Stephen C. Lundin, PhD., Harry Paul, and John Christensen, have detailed four philosophies, which I've paraphrased here:

Be there— Be emotionally present for people. It is the most powerful thing we can do for others. Show them how engaged and important they are to you.

Play— Tap into your natural way of being creative, enthusiastic, and having fun. At Pikes Fish Market, their customers are brought into the show.

Make Their Day— Find simple ways to delight people and make their day!

Choose your Attitude— Take responsibility for your attitude. Ask yourself the hard question, "Is my attitude helping or hurting my team?" Be super hyper aware of what you are projecting.

This newfound philosophy creates an environment where people love to come to work. It ignites a fire. It is a simple, predictable pathway to working together. It improves the overall trust and induces a teamwork dynamic second to none. It has transformed their climate. When you build great environments for people to gravitate toward, they will in turn attract patrons. It takes a lot of commitment to be a fishmonger. It is hard work, but also hard play. When your mission is to make others happy, you seem to forget how taxing your job is. You focus on attaining the results of bringing joy to others with every interaction. The endorphins will run wild, and you end up not focusing on the stinky fish, but on how you are able to make people feel.

Real estate transactions are not always seamless. In fact, there are inevitably going to be hiccups, stress, and fires to put out. When you are focusing on your people, alleviating their stress, and extending a servant-led customer service experience, your stress and frustrations can fade to the background of what really matters.

Treat your customers like humans, not patrons. Connect and focus on making others feel welcome and happy! Customers want to buy things from companies they connect to. Pike Place has absolutely nailed it.

When you go to their website, it is all about the stories of their customers. I don't see different kinds of fish and pricing. I see people SMILING as a result of the market's mission. The site encourages you to "share your story." I love this! Great organizations understand it is about the people and the art of telling their stories, not yours.

I LOVE GETTING BEHIND THE CAMERA AS MUCH AS I LIKE BEING IN FRONT OF IT.

When you pull people into a very interactive experience, magic happens. Creating fun and laughter induces an emotional connection that is so pure and leaves consumers craving more.

This philosophy has spawned a corporate training frenzy, with bestselling books in twelve languages. There was no plan for John to ever write, speak, and train other industries. It naturally evolved and has been a blessing to so many other companies. When I teach, I show a video of Pike Place and express the importance of creating a joy-filled experience, illustrating the power of being different. Pike Place customers, and those simply walking by witnessing the experience, do the marketing for this business.

Talk about a lasting impression! Six years after attending this class where I was introduced to Pike Place, and I am still raving and referring to this company! I am one of their marketers! I love to share and teach about their methodology and use their example as a tool to create an environment and experience like no other. Pick up the book, *Fish!: A Proven Way to Boost Morale and Improve Result*s. You can truly change the ecosystem and culture from the inside out with these principles.

I was listening to a podcast, *Business Done Differently* with Jesse Cole. I mention Jesse a lot. He is my spirit animal when it comes to barrier breaking and being different. He was interviewing the owners of an HVAC company. You think to yourself, how could an HVAC company do things really creatively? They have fulfilled the customer experience. Their company is called Icebound, Service Emperor. This incredible company is owned by Tersh and Julie Bissett. They do so many cool things. Their slogan is funny, yet impactful: Treating Your Customers Like Your Grandma

I won't go into their whole customer journey but will hit on the highlights that really anchored me. First of all, they give back to their community. They give a percentage of their sales to the Georgia Police K9 Foundation.

One of the things that they do on the front end is, whenever you call in or schedule a service call, one of the questions that you're going to be asked is, "What's the one item under $20 that you couldn't live without?" Most of the time, that's easy. "It's tacos. A Snickers bar," or something. This is a simple question but oh so powerful. They then keep detailed notes and for the next service call, send a Snickers or a certificate for a few tacos.

Some of the systems are automated to ensure the processes are operating as designed and nothing falls through the cracks. First, the customer will receive a message that the service expert is on his way. There is a picture of the service expert with a short, unique service story. It is similar to the Uber app where you can see where the technician is in real time. Second, they send a survey through text and email when they receive notification that the job is completed. It asks if your air conditioner is cooling and if you are happy with the service experts and install crews who performed the call.

I just spent three days on hold for over three hours with our internet/cable company trying to rectify a problem. I called three times due to being constantly disconnected while on the phone with an agent. The agents had my contact information, but not one of them attempted to return our call, knowing we were frustrated with the service and issues. They also have a prompt that tells you to use their text tech help for faster service. I did this simultaneously while on hold and no one answered until hours later. The tech finally came out and was not prepared to resolve our issue. He did not even bring an extra cable box. He said a tech would bring it out the next day from 3-5 p.m. The next day no one showed. These feelings of frustration are fresh in my mind. My main two complaints were hold time and feeling like I could not get a human to help me. Sure, technology is great, but not when I have a problem. We crave human-centered customer service. Second, I did not feel as though the service experts were prepared or knowledgeable enough to fix the issue. Lastly, I definitely did not think the company was empathetic for my time invested on hold, the fact there were no resolutions, and a no-show on opportunity number two for them to make it right. The third appointment we had a tech out and an hour later, we were back at square one. As loyal customers for over thirty years, we are now left feeling like we want to break up with this company and seek a company who appreciates us and will serve us at a high level.

By contrast, Icebound, Service Emperor has mastered customer care and alleviates customer frustration by their systems. They go above and beyond in so many ways. The service expert comes into the home and always puts booties on to respect the homeowner's home. They listen to the customer's overview of the issue and educate them accordingly. The expert has the latitude to go through the house thoroughly and itemize items under a certain amount to fix at no charge! How awesome is this? I love that we would have gotten a call or message right after the job was complete to ensure we had a positive experience. If I would have gotten a call directly afterwards with my service silliness, it would have eased the pain and the company could have turned it around.

Icebound then makes a happy call. Calling to just ensure the customer is happy and nothing could have been done differently is huge. You are validating your customer's opinion and encouraging feedback on how to improve. I don't know about you, but I love this. They then go a step further and offer a special treat that everyone adores. If you buy a new HVAC system, you get a massage. They have partnered with a local masseuse. When you get your happy call, you are informed you can set up a mobile massage with Mary. If I was offered a mobile massage, you can bet I would be posting and telling everyone I knew about this unique perk. Talk about a WOO experience! They also partner with a local cookie company and will send out surprise treats to customers. There is a 365-day system for all engagement above the first 100 days. This company is nailing it! And again, they are giving a level of service that gets people talking and doing the marketing for them.

Our clients are stressed. They are packing and moving. Their bodies are hurting, and they are emotionally exhausted from the whole process. Giving a mobile massage, even a chair massage, is really incredible! I would remember this far more than a welcome mat or kitchen knives.

Zappos is also known for their elite service. One of my favorite stories is when Zappos sent a baby blanket to the customer because they heard a baby crying in the background! You just sewed up a customer for life! The most memorable customer experiences are when you develop and connect on an emotional level. I heard a goosebump-worthy story that one of their customers was late sending back their return shoes due to a death. Zappos quickly credited the fee for the late return. The customer then received a stunning bouquet of flowers as an offering of condolence from the company. THIS is what it is about.

I pulled up in the driveway for one of my first dates with my husband. There were two motorcycles in the driveway. I was mortified. I hated motorcycles, but even more, I wanted to look good, and the wind creating a rat's nest effect in my hair is not my cup of tea. I was dreading his plan to go for a ride. Cue the hallelujah chorus, he has since sold his motorcycle. However, if I was in the market for a motorcycle, Harley Davidson has it down. Customers are encouraged to join an exclusive Harley Owners Group of about 325,000 owners and growing. This connects bikers to each other so they can develop a sense of community and hyper-local riding meetups. They have a beautiful way of creating pride in their brand and fostering the sense of elite and treasured ownership.

The Buffer app creates a unique approach. The customers are so much their focus, they have a support team called the Happiness Team. Their primary job is to engage and address questions and issues expeditiously in order to keep customers happy at all times. They seek to understand their consumers so they can tailor WOW moments.

We have Verizon wireless. One of the things I have recently noticed is their effort to write more to add value, such as offering business-centric webinars.

My dream job would be to sit in a think tank and come up with ideas on how to WOO, WOW, and create experiences that strike chords in a deep and powerful way. I am currently making that dream a reality. I often get calls and requests on how to be more creative and innovative in social media and other areas of customer service. I am creating a simple, single-page website with a menu of services I'll offer to those who want to hire me by the hour to jump in their think tank. I hope to add a massive value to other small businesses, offering ideas and quick action steps they can take in order to create a new pulse that will help them grow and be top of mind in their respective industries.

The best way to retrieve customer feedback is immediately after you deliver the product. Get it while it is fresh on their minds.

Consider post-interaction surveys and review links that can be delivered in real-time through programmed tools such as email or phone calls.

Starbucks, for example, often sends an email survey to their customers immediately after a store visit.

The survey asks customer-service questions specifically for the Starbucks location where they had just made a purchase. In the survey, they ask the customer to rank the friendliness of the baristas and speed of the service.

Our preferred photography company, Nested Tours, has started doing this as well on each transaction. The message it sends to us is that the company genuinely cares about each customer service experience and wants an opportunity to improve. This method is pleading for constructive criticism. When a company seeks to understand the consumer's needs, they want to exceed and over-deliver. Negative feedback is an invitation to grow, learn, and evolve through recognizing a weakness or hole in your organization.

You can learn so much from getting feedback. Giving permission for your customers to be transparently honest with you is powerful.

Observing customer service experiences is fascinating to me. I am always writing notes when I notice a goosebump moment. I can tell you I am way more impressed when there is an emotional connection and sentiment in the company's efforts to extend a stellar journey.

Jon Spoelstra, author of *Marketing Outrageously*, has a brilliant idea. He has a lot of experience as an executive for many NBA organizations. He pays his employees to go to an NBA game in another city. The goal is to bring back one fantastic idea to be able to adopt in your own business's experience plan. He encourages his employees to jot down five ideas a day. In ninety days, have a kick butt staff meeting to go over your ideas. Obviously, they all won't be good, but you prime your brain to be creative daily. You are always seeking ways to improve and enhance your experience for your customers.

You can plan a cruise, all-inclusive vacation, or Disney trip. Evaluate and anatomize your customer service experience. Take notes like you are a nerdy college student and report back your pros/cons and ideas to bring to the table to implement.

I challenge you to dissect your customer experience and note all the complaints and frustrations that have surfaced in your transactions to serve your families. What are the main pain points in your organization? Create a list and work out how you can reverse engineer your processes or protocols. Then commit to make the pain point a victory!

The message I want to convey is that no matter what industry you are in, you can stand out. We all must be keen at our crafts and experts in our field. But without our love for people, we don't have a business. People are our business. The sooner you as a business owner gets this, the sooner you will see customer service satisfaction rise. Why is just doing the status quo acceptable? I don't know about you, but my goal in any area of my life has not been to just get by or master mediocrity. Mediocrity is crowded, I want to master greatness.

You will hear me say we don't focus on our competition in our industry. We want to compete on our level of how we serve, not by copying competitors. We have always looked at ways we have personally been positively shocked with incredible, stellar customer service experiences. To this day, every time I hear an employee of any company say, "No problem," it makes me cringe. The difference in saying "My pleasure," is astronomical and changes my perception. When I hear, "No problem," I hear the person saying to me they will do the task or perform the service but not really be excited or jazzed about it. When I hear, "My pleasure," I hear it is an honor for them to serve me and they are happy to do it.

I was fortunate enough to work alongside a wonderful woman who I have been blessed to call my friend for the last fifteen years. If an employer could clone this lady's enthusiasm for serving others, they'd be rich. She answered her phone a hundred times a day, and every time, she answered the phone with the same enthusiasm. The person on the other end felt like it was the first time she had answered a call, not the fiftieth. She answered the phone, "Yukon High School, this is Sue. I can help you!" I loved this so much! Not only did she say those words, but she also smiled while saying them and she meant them. If someone was upset, this greeting already brought their stress down a couple of notches. They could hear that the person on the other end cared and was there to help or direct them in finding a solution. How rare is it that you are greeted with a human person on the other end who seems pumped and excited to serve you and your needs? I am hoping that customer service can rise up and bring back this core belief of serving others at the highest level.

SUE HINSON, MY BOTTLE OF SUNSHINE

I called a builder just yesterday and the receptionist kept repeating this phrase, "How can I be helpful?" It made me get all the tingles as I truly felt that she wanted to help me and go above and beyond.

In our business with our clients, we always seek to understand first. We don't ever claim to know it all. If we don't know something, we always leave them with the confidence we will get those answers for them. We always want to offer empathy during times of frustration and let them know we are working our best to offer a solution and a win/win for all parties. Being realtors, we can sometimes see the worst in people. It is almost like a bridezilla situation when you see your clients at rock bottom or under more stress than they can handle. It is our job to be all in. We are in this together. We will cheer and celebrate when appropriate, but we will kneel and lend a hand or compassionate ear to console the broken.

ANDREW, MEGAN AND I- WE ARE IN THIS TOGETHER!

Even celebration is often missed, skipped, or rushed over as we move onto the next thing. But without acknowledgement, our lives can easily become "one darned thing after another."

Isn't it just pathetic that it is not that hard to stand out and create the best service experience? If normal is being mediocre and not serving at a high level, I am tickled pink to be different. The normal service leaves consumers often feeling frustrated, hopeless, ready to sever ties, not more committed to a business. We all need to level up in this area and truly remember we are here to serve. That is a big word. It is to be taken seriously. In our market, there are approximately 10,000 realtors. When we receive that phone call to help people buy, sell, or invest, I take it very seriously. There are literally thousands of other real estate professionals they could call on. When our phone rings, there is not a single time I don't feel honored and humbled. I want to constantly remind them through our actions and service of why they were right in choosing to trust us with their largest investments.

Don't mistake a creative approach that is not supported by a fine-tuned strategic stream of systems in place. Models will create margin and longevity in this business before creativity can sustain it alone. ---- Denise Schroder

Adelina Rotar was essential in teaching me to not get distracted with creativity before establishing refined, polished systems. The systems are pivotal in being able to provide a well-rounded customer service experience.

We have continued to stay true to ourselves and prove that our marketing may seem out of the box or quirky and fun-spirited, but make no mistake, we get results. We perform at a high level and will continue to dominate the market as we never become complacent in providing anything but the most stellar customer service experience.

How do you stand out, and become and stay Top of Mind in a sea of realtors?

Be Fearlessly Authentic.

Be a Voice, not an Echo.

Be Creative.

Be Purposeful.

Be YOU

Be the Exception!

Who are You? What is your Brand?

What do people say about you?

What do you want them to say about you?

What are you willing to do to get them to say it?

Lean into your own image and unique viewpoint. Don't get caught up with the competition, be YOU!

Are your dreams bigger than other people's opinions or vice versa?

Tip: Position yourself as the town expert! Commit to building a float for the city parades. You can even invite your clients to come help you decorate it, ride in it, or walk behind it helping to hold signage! There are thousands that attend parades. What an awesome, fun way to get name recognition in the whole town.

For a local carnival, craft show, or local fair, give out branded balloons for the kids to walk around with all day. The goal is to get others to market for you. This is an inexpensive way to have your brand floating around quite purposefully.

Remember, being different is your superpower. What small acts or details can you add to your menu of service that alleviate a pain point or just extend kindness?

How can you exceed expectations and always deliver on your promise to leave your clients feeling they did win the jackpot by hiring you?

Develop these ideas into your business model and have all your employees implement them. Have a unified message from the top down.

Chapter 10
Content Creation

I married when I was twenty-two years old. With my small-town mentality, I yearned for the white picket fence and a baby to carry on each hip. My dream was to be a mom and a little Miss Making-it-from-scratch-Betty Crocker. So many things did not end like I envisioned. Shortly after I had my second baby, I began to feel things were off physically. My normal energy level puts the energizer bunny to shame, but something had changed. When I would talk to doctors, I would be encouraged to just take an antidepressant. As a stay-at-home mother, Oprah was a ritualistic fixture in my living room every day at 4 pm. I decided to put my story writing skills to the test to get some help and guidance from the mother of all gurus, Oprah! I mean isn't she the first person you think of when you want expert advice? In 1999, I wrote into the Oprah Winfrey Show. I was very desperate and expressive, to say the least. I wanted to *show* Oprah my story, not just *tell* it. I had one shot to clearly articulate, through a carefully crafted string of words, my dilemma. My vulnerability would help others and that is what drove me to put myself out there.

I was in shock to get a call from one of the lead producers at Harpo Studios, Mary Donahue, the day after I had emailed. She chatted with me like we were familiar old friends, then asked if I could give my husband-at-the-time a warning: she would also be calling him in a measly five minutes. I was petrified at how he would respond to an insane call like this. The next thing I knew, they flew a production crew out to film us for eight hours. I was thinking what the heck am I supposed to pretend to do, acting like the crew is not crouched in the corner of my living room and there were no blinding light boxes in our faces? That was my first taste of TV and the power of storytelling. Can I just say, I was hooked. We had a full day of filming the kids play, helping me clean the house, baking cookies – which I never did in real life because I burn everything I cook. Very soon, we were set to be whisked away to Harpo Studios in Chicago to film our show.

Going on The Oprah Winfrey show was about as big of an audience as I could have dreamt of having. After the birth of my second child, I was hearing my doctors tell me I was just depressed. I knew in my gut that was not it. I did not want to be put in a stereotypical box. I knew my body and just wanted someone to take the extra time and sincerely listen to me. I wanted my hormones checked but was told two different times I was just feeling some light postpartum symptoms. I did not want to take an antidepressant. I honestly did not feel like I was being diagnosed before being offered a prescription. I was not okay with being prescribed a pill that could alter so many things and have possible side effects, especially when in my gut I knew it was not the right call for me. Oprah's producer set it up for my labs to be drawn and the process rushed. They ran all kinds of tests on me, and finally revealed I had little to NO testosterone. This was an amazing revelation and turned out to be an accurate, easy fix to get me back to my old self. The show was titled "Women Who Don't Want Sex." That was a creative title and one that let's just say gave people something to talk about! My mother was mortified I was going on not just national television, but the Oprah Winfrey show to talk about sex, or not having sex. Either way, the word "sex" was a subject leaving her to blush versus boast about my TV debut.

Oftentimes, when you are a guest on a show, you are seated in the front row and the cameras simply pan to you for your time to answer questions directed to you. However, I was seated on stage next to Oprah the entire show. I felt like her right-hand woman! This was one of the moments in my life I wish I had savored more. I can remember her doing some kind of hand signals under her chair and a shoe fairy literally slipped a different pair of black and white mules under her chair, her having the top button of her pants unbuttoned, and the entire time, giving off a calming aura I can't explain. She whispered to me, "You are here because you have a gift of storytelling in such an honest and transparent way. Just pretend we are in my living room having a girl chat."

My nerves calmed and I was ready to share my truth and *show* my story to empower women to speak up, that we know our bodies better than anyone, and no one can advocate better than we can. If we don't stand up for ourselves, no one will. The show ratings did so well I was asked back for a six-month follow-up episode. When I called, the producer told me that the fact that viewers, as well as Oprah herself, wanted an update from my journey was huge, showing the relevance of this topic. Little did I know that a desperate cry and articulate, well-written letter from a small-town girl to Oprah Winfrey would lead to sharing a mutual issue I knew affected and impacted women all over the world. This was truly surreal!

People want to know your story. They want to be shown who you are, more than be told bare facts about you. Back then, when we wanted to share our story, we called Oprah. In today's modern world, we go to social media!

Social media has been instrumental in us exponentially growing our name recognition and branding. I have to admit, it is scary sometimes to hope you get a good reception from all the content you curate and put out into the universe. It is easy to take it personally when you are the one doing the creating. Being authentically YOU is the key to connecting with others on a deeper level.

Also remember, social media is a two-way street!

Whether you are trying to accomplish brand building, leave a footprint in leadership, find speaker engagement opportunities, get exposure, or ramp up your social media influence, you must have a plan. Social media is intentional! Don't grasp at straws and chase the wind! Be purposeful in what content you post!

You have daily items on your schedule to prioritize certain things in your business. Your social media strategy needs to be just as deliberate.

I have so many ideas that pop into my head twenty-four hours a day. I have a note section in my phone and a photo folder with all my ideas saved. I also have a notebook where I jot down tons of ideas, including details on if I need to purchase or find any items for different photo shoots we do for posts. I believe in batch marketing. I schedule at least a week in advance. I have a general topic focus every day of the week, but I can easily deviate from that when an opportunity arises to spontaneously grab fresh, hot, in-the-moment content! Sometimes something for the day may change if there is trending news that would create a popular topic. You want to post in real time, while the topic is hot!

CLICKBAIT: WILL SMITH/CHRIS ROCK

Some people are petrified of social media! Don't let it stump you. Come up with a simple plan and stick to it.

Who are you?

What do you want to be known for?

What is your message?

What is your brand?

Jot down your interests, hobbies, and mission.

My hobbies are interior design, remodel/transformation projects, fashion, creating comedic memes, spending time with family, and selling real estate. Yours may be gardening, landscaping, reading, running, yoga, family time, real estate, or painting! People love short videos. Content is all around you. Once you get out of your own head, it gets easier. I am coaching a client now to create her own voice on social media. She has an interior design business and also remodels homes. She truly is the hardest working woman. She gets in there and will attempt anything a man would do. She gets sick to her stomach when I put her on the spot! I don't want to give her time or the choice to NOT just do it! Her fear is not being perfect in her social media presence efforts. She gets nervous and sometimes second guesses herself. This is such a common feeling for so many. I struggle with it now at times, too. Some haters will take opportunities to make passive aggressive comments when I am being vulnerable. It is okay that not everyone likes you or responds the way you envisioned. There are always going to be those kinds of people. We have nearly 5,000 friends on Facebook. They are NOT all nice and unfortunately, they are not all our true friends. You must develop a thick skin when you put yourself out there. My first client, Angel, has just recently started posting videos at her latest remodel job! We went over creating bite-size content and making video a priority. Now she has done short videos on how to texture a wall, pick out granite countertops, and presented some of her design products. She is getting a lot of exposure organically and eventually I think she will even start to enjoy it and rid herself of the nerves surrounding her content! You are selling yourself and your image you project! Let people see who they would be hiring!

My content includes things I am passionate about and that are my hobbies! Interior design, cooking, gardening, family, kids, thrifting, crafting, fashion, and friends.

Another thing to remember is people LOVE talking about themselves. Even when you post about yourself, invite engagement! ENGAGE, ENGAGE, ENGAGE!

FISHING AND READING MILLIONAIRE REAL ESTATE AGENT

Having one hundred and six likes and one hundred and twenty engagement comments is a success, friends. I made an announcement of a special anniversary date of me becoming a realtor. But…I was able to turn it around and make it about my audience by asking how long they had been at their jobs. Engagement WINS every time, and it is so much more fun to learn and engage with others than to just post and run, sharing something people scroll by and glaze over.

Check out this kitchen post of a hideous purple explosion. It got astronomical engagement! Two hundred and eighty-two comments is incredible! And guess what, you need to interact with each and every comment in some way! You can like their comment, but it is much more personal to interact in a deeper way than simply a like.

 Denise N Troy Schroder   •••
1d • ⚙

Describe this kitchen in ONE word!!! Don't cheat!!!!

😍👍😮 34   282 Comments

STOP THE SCROLL AND ASK OPINIONS.
EVERYONE HAS ONE!

Here is an example of an easy plan to follow:

Monday: Engagement Design/Real Estate.

Tuesday: Transformation Tuesday (post fun before/after remodels or your own DIY craft transformations), Customer Spotlights, BAB (means Boost another Business), Inspirational Quotes.

I even created a free logo when I post my own DIY design dupe projects!

DESIGN ON A DIME LOGO FOR MY
CRAFTING/THRIFTING POSTS

Go through your sphere of influence and offer to do a video post or testimonial. Ask what they need in their business for it to thrive more. Help them get this message out, and if they need help, guide them in articulating it. We don't just post it on our social media platforms. We tag the business and post it on all our private real estate pages, groups, local marketplaces, and then follow up with them to see if it brought business. We did this last week for a mobile detailer, and within twenty minutes he had two new customers. I put him on the spot after reading his very gregarious personality. He just told me a little bit about his menu of services and his contact information and had my car looking sleek and immaculate for his proof in the pudding. It was so little effort for us to be able to help him grow his business. It feels good to help someone build and grow when you are like minded.

Wednesday: Wacky Wednesday (funny TikToks we have made, blooper moments, meme mimic photos something with humor) Engagement (a personal question that allows your audience to share their opinion).

NOT MANY PEOPLE HAVE A GIANT PHOTO OF THEIR HUSBAND GRACING THEIR SWIMSUIT. HE LOVES IT!

REAL ESTATE IS ALWAYS ON MY MIND,
EVEN WHEN I AM BASKING.

UNIQUE EXPERIENCES ARE SUCH A FUN WAY TO
ENGAGE YOUR AUDIENCE

Thursday: Throwback Thursday/Meme Mimic (this is a new series we have been doing and it is so much fun! I can spend a whole day doing batch marketing for this niche).

Friday: Local and Community (What's Happening in your City, so easy to find local events that are going on. Always tag the business and show your support for them).

Saturday: Family/In the moment posts or Craft ideas for kids. (This gets a lot of engagement).

COOKING LESSONS WITH COCO AND JUDAH

Sunday: Quick Designer Fashion tip (I partner with my friend Angel! She coincidentally was our first client, as has been mentioned throughout the book. We cross-promote and will do a video on a transformation she has done to a room or home, a quick tip, or walk through a flip or remodel she has going on. These types of posts are wildly well-received.) I have been known to demonstrate how to jackhammer tile in stilettos, it can be quite entertaining!

Always have a high energy and sense of humor when distributing content! Make people want to watch your videos until the very end by keeping them entertained. If you love inspirational quotes, make a day you post one that resonates with you. You could step it up one step further and do a video about how the quote helps you or makes you feel!

Seasonally, we try to mix it up and do different things to continue to level up and differentiate ourselves. This year I am going to be a human "elf on a shelf" for some quirky, unique posts! I am so looking forward to the creativity on this and will employ our grandson to wear a matching elf suit to be integrated into this fun series.

I have also become known in my Facebook/Instagram circle as the fashion critic! I post regularly on the best/worst dressed in fashion on the red carpet. I will have friends private message asking when my fashion rundown list is coming out. I have been so consistent with this, that people have grown to expect it. I have about twenty friends/clients who engage with these posts!

Tip: If you get stumped, google top things trending and search for what "National" day it is. Seems every day is a nationally recognized day for something. Today for example, August 19th, is National Potato Day! Who knew?

All my design-centric, funny, and strange real estate siting posts remind my audience what we do for a living. Without having to force feed to everyone we are realtors, they know by the nature of our posts. The recipe is finding that balance to remind people what you do, the result being that they recognize you as the Number One Realtor of choice, as the one who comes top of mind in all things real estate.

Kids are one of my favorite things to post about! I have the absolute cutest children in our family. I am always taking a spontaneous video of them in action or catching them saying the darndest things! Who does not enjoy a baby giggle or me giving a famous lipstick tutorial to my nieces?

KIDS ARE A HIT ON SOCIAL MEDIA,
THE CUTER THE BETTER!

Don't overcomplicate it! You can come up with your topics and create your guide for a daily theme to post. It can truly be exhausting to keep up with all the changes that constantly occur on all the social media. Focus on one and start small! Our audience is online, social media platforms are your live stage! Give them the content that you get a standing ovation for!

The content we share is organically just us. Our goal is to have our audience feel like they are on a journey with us through highs and lows and doing life with us. We aren't just fronting an image that we manufactured based on what we think would inflate our sales volume.

Our audience is not being sold to; we are not shamelessly bragging to them. We are just stripped down and not afraid to make fun of ourselves. We can be vulnerable and pride ourselves in making others smile and laugh, creating WOO moments and story showing. We are down to earth and approachable. When people see our name scroll on their newsfeed they always smile!

I personally post five to ten times a day on my stories on Instagram and Facebook. This is a running play by play of our day and life! You never know what the day will bring, but be assured, I am there with my camera, ready to catch the moments. My castmates on the Food Network joke that no one even needs paparazzi when I am around. I do not let moments go uncaptured! I keep a folder on my phone marked social media content to stay stocked up!

There are many resources out there to help you get in a rhythm of putting out quality content that ultimately brings community and optimal engagement. Google is your best friend when you are stumped and have a brain freeze!

The 5-5-5 rule is simple and easy to do! You comment five times, send five DMs, and leave five likes! Easy enough, right?

Some of my favorite tools for high quality content creation are:

Canva: Canva is a graphic design platform that allows users to create social media graphics, presentations, posters, fliers, documents, and other visual content. Users can choose from many professionally designed templates, then edit the designs and upload their own photos through a drag and drop interface. I use the free version. What a great arsenal of DIY marketing collateral at your fingertips. Talk about a WOW factor! There are some stunning designs that will knock your socks off. I use Canva for so many things (logos, presentations, social media posts, fliers, infographics, etc.) that are visually pleasing. Being in such a visual-centric world of marketing, presentation matters. Canva makes me look good and people tend to think I have a professional designer. The templates are so incredible.

Befunky: I love befunky.com and PicMonkey.com too for quick collages! They are super user friendly! On PicMonkey, I can easily spray tan myself, which is a plus!

Tread lightly when you set up automation. Consumers crave human-centric interactions, not robotics. We are in the business of people, not digitizing everything for time management purposes. For example, I often distribute different content to LinkedIn and Twitter. I have it set up so that anything posted on my business page will syndicate out to LinkedIn. (Or at least similar content - in a different format we often have to adjust or trim the text due to character max rules). Our personal Facebook and Instagram content is very similar, however. They are both geared toward doing life with us and spritzing in real estate in fun and inspiring ways. We don't post content that our clients would be offended by or uncomfortable with! If I want to send something more edgy, I do it privately. A lot of our content is over the top, but never in a politically charged or sexually explicit way.

There are many scheduling programs too. My favorite is IFTTT—If This, Then That! You can set what they call recipes on this program. IFTTT is the free way to do more with hundreds of the apps and devices you love, including Twitter, Dropbox, Evernote, Nest, Fitbit, Amazon Alexa, and Google Assistant.

It is an easy way to automate tasks that might otherwise be repetitive or unable to talk to each other. It works like this: users are guided through a process to make simple scripts, (aka recipes), where some type of event in one device or service automatically triggers an action in another. IFTTT is also completely free, and well supported. There are now more than 300 channels — which are what you reference when creating recipes — spread across a range of devices and services, including social networks, smart appliances, smart home systems, and devices such as weather stations, audio systems, and wearables.

Later.com also has a free platform and is very popular. Hootsuite has rave reviews, but I believe there is a charge for the service.

Don't forget that posts that did well and generate memories are a great reason to repurpose content. We do this all the time and I speak about it later in a future chapter.

There are so many tools that simplify this big elephant we call social media. YOU can do it! Find one platform you want to hyper focus on and become an expert!

Take the focus off you and make it about the art of "story-showing," (this word may soon be added to Webster's dictionary). Stories will stick with people and are the vibration of connecting with others. I am not just on social media for likes, I am there to get to know people, engage, and connect on a deeper level.

Develop your own craft and style of storytelling in your content creation efforts and you will be amazed at the rewarding results. When people scroll your timeline, they should feel like they are getting a genuine sense of who you are and what you are about!

I AM RELENTLESSLY ALWAYS ON THE HUNT
FOR MY NEXT PHOTO OP.

Chapter 11
Facebook = GOLDMINE

Facebook is an absolute gold mine! What would I do without Facebook? I often wonder what people did before social media, seriously! This platform is the gift that keeps on giving! You have the opportunity to be a micro-influencer, offer value, humor, and tell a story. You are the star of your own show! I have found so many things I can do within this platform that are part of my daily and hourly marketing plan. Facebook has been a place where we have done so much brand recognition building for little to no cost. It is an open door into thousands of people's lives. It gives us a platform that is free for the most part to share, impact, influence, connect, build relationships, and market ourselves and our businesses. The magnitude of this platform is underrated by so many who operate small businesses. The reason why I say this is so many professionals don't act like Facebook is indeed a stage and you are in the spotlight. Don't just show up, show up and perform! Many people take to Facebook to passive aggressively say negative things about people, complain about service or businesses, flaunt too much skin, or celebrate their booze and party lifestyle. Facebook is your resume. Your Facebook timeline says so much about you. I call it speed dating. I can go on someone's Facebook and within five minutes have a feel for their character, who they are, their hobbies, what kind of people they interact with, and who they relate to and associate themselves with daily. When you think critically of what you simply view as a harmless post when you are angry, lost your marbles or sensibilities, or gain bravery induced by a late-night glass of wine, you may think differently about what you put out on social media. With screenshotting, nothing is ever gone or deleted. I have friends come to me for a social media audit. I encourage you all to do this. Scrub your social media and ask others to give you feedback on their honest, unfiltered perception of how you come off on all your social media profiles. When you have a date and you were connected on a dating site or referred by a friend, the first thing most do is investigate or creep through their Facebook. We get told by nearly all potential clients that we were investigated before being selected to interview for the opportunity to handle their largest investment.

Algorithms, rules, and regulations will change on all these social media platforms often. One thing remains, the common goal is to use these platforms to maintain relationships and make connections.

First, you must have friends for Facebook to actually work. We have nearly 5,000 friends, but if you don't use your social media as a tool to deepen relationships, it does not matter how many friends you have. Interaction is a two-way street.

Facebook serves as a digital meeting place where we can actively, organically build relationships and literally be alerted by the contact we are connecting with. We can keep up with people that ordinarily we would have completely lost touch with. Because we are in the relationship business, our clients become our friends and truly our tribe.

We add all of our clients to our friends on our personal Facebook. We do this because our clients become our friends through our process and relationship we build. Our personal page is where we connect. We want others to see who we really are and do life alongside us. We regularly post on our business page, but our interaction and engagements come from sharing and doing life with our Facebook friends. Our business page seems to be more informative. We can boost posts, but where we genuinely connect is through our personal page. We don't post anything on our page that is controversial or offensive. We are never trying to start social media wars over differing opinions in religion, politics, pandemic, etc. We don't use social media to passive aggressively send cryptic messages to anyone who does not like us or support us. We certainly aren't venting and bashing other businesses. We want our page to be a place where you are inspired, entertained, and encouraged. We want to do what we do with all our clients, and that is spread joy and laughter at any given opportunity. And yes, it is an opportunity to stop the scroll and give someone a chuckle or make them smile. There is nothing greater!

Notification Alerts:

When connecting with our clients, past and present, we set them up on Facebook for notifications. We want to see every time they post so we don't miss out on important things in their lives. I don't have time to scroll through and search 4,500–moving up to 5,000–friends, so this feature is incredible. I only comment, post on their walls, comment sections, or send a card when I genuinely feel led to do so… This has helped me so much to be in tune and quickly reference notifications to pay attention to.

Let's take a trip down memory lane! Repurposing good content is such a beautiful thing! I probably take more pictures than anyone. My family will tell you I drive everyone to drinking with the fact that everything is a photo op. I look at things through a creative lens. Endearing memories are such an amazing feature and a tool I use daily. The unique and creative photos we take with these families raise retrospective memories of how much they appreciated and enjoyed the customer service experience we provided. Take them back to that special celebratory day.

When we go through the buying or selling process, we use many opportunities to build memories. We often have a "Sold in how many days" sign and we incorporate the family when convenient. We also take photos at the closing table in true unforgettable fashion, and in front of the house in full celebratory fashion! When a memory pops up a year later, we always use this gem to reconnect with our clients and start a conversation of "Remember when?" or "Can you believe it has been a whole year?"

Another great tip is saving a photo of each family you serve, either in front of the house they purchased, or your celebratory closing day picture. At the end of the year, create a slideshow or reel. You can also do a year-end review, post each photo representing the family served/home closed, and "tag" each person. This is a great way for people to be tagged and reminded of their amazing experience and also see how many families you serve.

LILLI AND COLE BARNES: ONE OF THE MANY SURPRISE PROPOSALS WE HAVE FACILITATED ON CLOSING DAY.

I AM SUCH A SUCKER FOR LOVE! I CARRY MY WEDDING VEIL EVERYWHERE I GO!

EMMA AND GARRETT IN FULL CELEBRATION MODE

THE DYER KIDS JUMPED RIGHT INTO THE SPOTLIGHT.
KIDS LOVE PROPS!

BUYING YOUR FIRST HOME AT ANY AGE IS AMAZING.
BILL WAS ECSTATIC!

When we are helping clients purchase homes, we often take fun pics while on the hunt and especially when we go under contract, as well as closing day in front of the house, and at the closing table, etc.

TEST DRIVING THE TUBS IS A THING!

Don't underestimate this being a powerful way to reconnect and start a conversation. The memory most often reflects a very happy, joyous day they want to positively reminisce about in the future. It also reminds them of you and that you are still in their life! Being in your sphere, they will always be in your tribe as long as you nurture them, love them and don't let them forget how amazing you are, and more importantly, the service you provide. Real estate is not always happy, though, as you know. It is not always the elated first-time buyer, a newlywed couple, or a family moving up. Oftentimes, we are being invited into the situation due to a job loss, a physical or financial change, or physical limitation instigating a downsize or move to assisted living, even death or divorce. We are extremely sensitive to the fact that selling a childhood home because both your parents recently passed is not a happy time and do not post forced marketing photos. Each and every situation is so very different, and we are hypersensitive to each client's needs.

Facebook is also a place where people inevitably spill the tea. It is a common place where people go to vent, complain, gallivant around scantily clad, and sometimes even bully. Be very aware of how you present yourself online. Would you offend your grandma if she saw the content you post? Your Facebook page is your own personal billboard about yourself. People often get vulnerable on social media. We look to our community to support us, walk hand in hand with us, back us up, validate us, and sometimes even invite a little debate and banter. We mourn, we celebrate, we acknowledge, we share, (some overshare). At times you may feel like a post would be something someone would say to their therapist or a trusted confidante or bartender.

When our friends, family, or clients post something noteworthy, I jot it down. There may be the death of a loved one, a family pet, a new job, a job loss, a baptism, a personal goal met (i.e., first marathon completed), a graduation, or a cry for help or encouragement. I have always been someone that loves to give words of affirmation to others. It is one of my top love language needs, so I love to give and offer to others what naturally fills my cup. A handwritten card seems to be a lost art form. I will expand on this in a later chapter. I actually enjoy writing and sending cards, so this is not a chore on my to-do list. Change your mindset, this is a "get to do" for people. I want to show authentic care, concern, or celebrate in their wins.

One of my favorite ways to feel rewarded is to help others grow. When your sole purpose is being of service to others, your perspective shifts. If we got up every day, put pom-poms in our back pockets, get ready to help others, and clap and cheer when they win, our day would be so much fuller. How can you evangelize for others the way we want that reciprocated? You will attract what you are, and the law of reciprocity is magical. We have had the honor to find excellent service providers and build our businesses together, as well as help others grow at an exponential speed to reach their financial goals and create more jobs in the process. We have successfully been able to partner and grow others in areas such as handyman, plumbers, electricians, builders, lenders, home/termite inspectors, pest control, movers, structural engineers, designers, stagers, roofers, physicians, CPAs, and the list goes on.

I love the tag feature. Any time we recommend someone on Facebook or any social medium, we tag them. We also follow that up with a text and email pointing out that we referred to them so they can take a look at the post. This is done so they don't miss an opportunity to connect with a new prospect. We actively ask for reviews from our clients, so make certain you give reviews of all your favorite vendors. This to me is what it is all about. It is the reason why one of my and Troy's next steps has been to become real estate and small business coaches. Helping others tackle their fears, implement action plans that ultimately create growth, give security, bolster self-esteem and gain financial freedom is beyond elevating. Moving from proving yourself in your life or career into what your true purpose is in making a difference is a game changer. Real estate has been the vehicle by which we have exponentially grown, and it has opened so many doors to continue to push ourselves in all areas of life.

Seek to be a good finder on social media. There is an overabundance of trolls and negative energy on social media. Be a positive voice and do not ever underestimate the power of simple, kind words extended to others. When you feel it, say it! Connections and relationships are built on building others up, on being there when someone has fallen and needs help or an open ear.

We also use Facebook to market all our listings! We post them all on our business page (and boost the listing) and marketplace. Facebook Marketplace is a digital marketplace where users can arrange to buy, sell, and trade items with other people in their area. We don't necessarily track metrics of sales resulting from Marketplace. There are a lot of casual browsers on Facebook who are not truly in the market to buy, or not pre-approved, or who could not even buy a Schwinn bicycle. However, if given the opportunity, we can help convert anyone interested in purchasing to get connected with our preferred lenders and start the process seamlessly. The reason behind us posting on Marketplace, and also all the other private, hyperlocal groups with literally thousands and thousands of members, is simple. It is about reach and exposure establishing the perception that we are the local experts. I want the general public to see we have market share. We list and sell a lot of homes. We want to be a hyperlocal digital mayor of all things real estate. We have used this approach as part of our brand building, creating name recognition for quite some time. I don't just post the listing photos. I include a sharp collage with our photo and contact information so at the end of the photos it is anchored. It is a Schroder Listing! I use this same collage every time for continuity. It is eye-catching, with our colors and branding! It also has our hashtag and our short, concise mission statement. "We serve like we are chosen."

Also, with broker compliance needing to list our brokerage, all the contact information, etc., this is a sharp way to display the required information without distracting by having text all over our listing photos.

Implementing these easy ways to keep track and elevate engagement is a must! Facebook is a powerful platform to connect in an organic way on a daily basis with our database!

LOGO MARKETING PIECE FOR SOCIAL MEDIA
(CREATED ON CANVA)

Chapter 12
The Lost Art of Handwritten Notes

Reading Gary Chapman's book, *The 5 Love Languages: The Secret to Love that Lasts*, I've found that one of my love languages is definitely "Words of Affirmation." When you suggest to your children, husband, or yourself to write handwritten thank you cards, universally there is push-back. This is just not the case for me. I love doing it, and know it is such a lost art form. I rarely ever receive handwritten cards. When I do, I save them, and it truly means so much, especially in this day and age of sending a simple, sterile text, email, Facebook direct message, etc. A cheesy text or Facebook message can often feel void of genuine gratitude. There is something so much more meaningful when I know someone sat down and authentically took the time to write to me by hand, address it, stamp it the old-school way, and get it to the mailbox. When you can wake up every day and ask yourself how you can touch someone and make a difference today, your perspective shifts. Have a go-giver mentality and look for ways and opportunities people need to be ministered to. Sometimes sending a card to someone saying you are proud of them is incredible. You may be the only cheerleader they have celebrating them. I used to minimize my impact on how to be vulnerable and open to just a few minutes a day. I began to spend real time focused only on finding someone who needed a smile, or on empowering someone else. At first, I thought I was blessing them, but it ended up blessing me.

Social media gives us an inside look at people's lives. We see causes for celebration, experience empathy, seek prayer, and sometimes see a cry for help. Scrolling news feeds is intentional for me. I want to know everyone's story, and everyone has a story!

YOUR NEWSFEED IS YOUR STAGE. SEEK TO SEE WHAT OTHERS ARE SPOTLIGTING IN THEIR LIVES.

I am not going to focus on silliness or be distracted by interpersonal drama, but if someone lost a loved one or a pet, graduated college, received a promotion, celebrated an anniversary, had a death of a loved one, I want to know! Celebrating with your tribe and kneeling with them when they fall is so pivotal and just as important. Social media can make relationships seem surface level or superficial. We have to make the extra effort to take the cues of their lives to connect and continue our relationships. Which brings me to this point right here! I set all of our clients up to follow them and receive notifications when they post something on their timeline. This way, it is easier for me to keep up when I want to interact or be prompted or moved to send a card, extend a phone call, or simply reply on the thread. On a side note, you can also categorize them into groups so if you only wish to post to certain people, they are organized in the group. This is not a technical how-to book, but all the things I am suggesting are tech for dummies!

To me, my most treasured part of my business is that everyone has a story. I love getting to see children grow and people succeed, or knowing when someone needs extra love and encouragement, or expresses a physical or emotional need. I use social media to be notified of events and precious moments, but my interaction is in a much deeper, connective way than just being a normal social media creeper. It is just a tool so I can stay in touch with people I truly care about and want to continue to feed that relationship. Our database is large, so it is easy for past clients to get lost. My goal is for no one to be left behind.

Today I went to the mailbox with a stack of cards to send out. Before sealing the envelopes, I usually add some metallic streamer or confetti for a celebratory card. I sent two condolence cards, a recovery card, a pet loss card, and a congratulatory card for a recent graduation. This is a daily thing I do and a way I can minister to others through encouragement. I hope that these handwritten cards mean as much to the recipients as when I personally receive one.

HANDWRITTEN LETTERS

My mother turned fifty, and we had a huge party for her right after she was diagnosed with cancer. The greatest gift she ever received in her life, she said, were personal notes people wrote to her and brought to the party. We collected so many, and they brought more joy than any trinket or gift could ever offer.

What can you do today to bring someone joy or relief?

How can you simply spread joy and kindness with words?

I challenge you to send a quick text or write a short postcard or note. You may never begin to realize the impact this small effort will have. Sometimes the little things add up to make the biggest difference in someone else's life. If you think it, say it!

> # "BE SOMEBODY WHO MAKES EVERYBODY FEEL LIKE SOMEBODY."

Book reference: *The 5 Love Languages: The Secret to Love that Lasts* by Gary Chapman

Chapter 13
Happy Birthday

I don't know a single person on earth that does not like to be celebrated. Again, Facebook makes it easy to prompt us to make a phone call, make a video, send a text, post on a wall, send a direct message. It is like a built-in assistant. One of the first things I do in the morning is check the birthday list on Facebook. In my case, I go a step further at times and have been known to send a sing-a-gram. For a select few occasions I have been known to take my birthday sing-a-gram to the streets and deliver it in person!

There is simply NO way to forget someone's birthday! Facebook is there as a daily cheat sheet to refer to. As backup, make certain you save your client's birthdays in your CRM to send a snail mail card. We have birthday reminders in our CRM for a week before so cards can also be mailed. For social media purposes, we do something a little different. We send either a branded, fun, personalized GIF birthday message, or taking it one step further, a sing-a-gram of me singing the Marilyn Monroe version of Happy Birthday! I have people EXPECT these sing-a-grams once they have received one. It is different, branded to me, and stands out among all the other monotonous messages they receive in droves.

I just had a birthday this week. Literally hundreds of people gave me a birthday wish. I responded to every single message, thanking them. However, MOST people do not even see every message, as they get grouped and buried on your timeline. Do something rare and exclusive! Be memorable, be different. Send them a message or picture that is not vanilla, easily dismissed and forgotten. Anytime you make contact with others, you want the effort, sentiment, or thought to anchor with them. Take the extra time to express something personal about them in your message. Taking a couple extra seconds to make something more personal speaks volumes.

If you can't sing—No EXCUSES—download the free Dubsmash app, or the Snapchat app (use the voice modifier for a quirky effect) and send a fun video your client won't soon forget. You need to not just stop the scroll but evoke emotions. Oftentimes, people get hundreds of birthday messages posted in mere vanilla, formal, obligatory style. BE DIFFERENT! Do something they won't forget! You can always step up your game and send a $5 or $10 Starbucks card through Facebook. If you want to know what someone's favorite things are, such as music, restaurants, etc., refer to their ABOUT page on Facebook. Look at their check-ins, sports teams, movies, books, and see what pages they like for deep intel into what would be a perfect and thoughtful gift. We have a personalized card sending service we just discovered. We can send a gift card along with the snail mail card and the system is super simple! You have to pay monthly for www.AMCARDS.COM, but it has so many fun features to simplify making unique, warm touches to your tribe. I love how AMCARDS branding allows you to customize the default back panel of your greeting cards. You can use your logo or whatever you want! The cards are sharp and use high quality paper! You can easily upload your database or just send it to individual folks.

Go the extra mile, take the extra seconds to go above and beyond in an exclusive way.

BIRTHDAY SOCIAL MEDIA POSTS

Crazy enough, as I said before, sometimes I do in-person, live, impromptu sing-a-grams. This particular occasion was a client's fiftieth birthday celebration. I showed up at the house and made my way to the birthday boy! The reaction was priceless from the recipient and all his family and friends that were present. The smiles, laughs and energy evoked by this sing-a-gram was so rewarding! What do you think I did next? I then provided a human-interest story to the local paper, and they happily published it. It was that simple! It was a fun, unique, feel-good, heartwarming story about an administrator in the school system. Your cities are always looking for great content. Why not be the one to supply them with some fantastic local happenings. I can also send a video and the response is always so fantastic!

This is the biggest smile I have ever seen on my friend Mike's face! Talk about feeling honored and special His face says it all and made it so worth the effort!

'Marilyn' Surprise

Mike Workman, Yukon Public Schools' director of maintenance, was surprised for his 50th birthday party with a special birthday impersonation act by Marilyn Monroe AKA Denise Schroder. She was

MARILYN MONROE IS ALIVE AND WELL,
STILL MAKING THE NEWS!

"Don't just focus on stopping the scroll, focus on evoking emotions."

Chapter 14
Make the Most of Holiday Posts

Is it possible to have too much fun at work? We have an absolute blast with holiday posts. Holiday posts are a fun way to be really quirky and unique in approach on social media. While scrolling it can seem mundane seeing your newsfeed filled to the brim with cookie cutter posts. here are examples of just a few of the ways we have spruced up our feed for the holidays to stop the scroll!

We submitted our Valentine's pic to be posted and featured on the local billboard! What a cool way to get noticed and create fantastic social media content.

LOCAL VALENTINE'S BILLBOARD

FIND CREATIVE WAYS TO POST AROUND EACH AND
EVERY HOLIDAY

St. Patty's Day is a day many love to celebrate!

ST. PATTY'S DAY PHOTO

On Easter it is fun to highlight Easter Egg hunts and in this case the World's Ugliest Easter Cake that I made that the family was NOT impressed with. I am okay posting things and being quite self-deprecating.

WORLD'S UGLIEST EASTER CAKE

MY DISGRUNTLED, SWEET NIECE ON THE HUNT

On Halloween, we actually dress up and go to our closings in costume! We have such a blast being a kid on this cool holiday! Our clients and title company employees absolutely eat it up and now expect it! How can you add joy and a smile to those around you?

WE LOVE RUNNING AROUND TOWN ON HALLOWEEN
SUITED UP AS SUPERHEROS

DELIVERING LAUGHS EVERYWHERE WE GO! I DO NOT RECOMMEND DRIVING IN THESE SUMO SUITS! THEY ARE BUILT IN AIR BAGS, THOUGH!

IMPERSONATING BLAKE SHELTON AND GWEN STEFANI
GOT US SOME STARES.

December is my favorite month! I love seeing all the mischief our Elf
on the Shelf can get into as well as other Christmas traditions!

ELF ON THE SHELF SHENANIGANS

KEEPING IT CLASSY CHRISTMAS CARD COMPLIMENTS
OF CANE'S

Chapter 15
Nix the Highlight Reel

My perspective shift now is that selling homes is a byproduct of what we do. We are in the business of serving people. We don't sell houses, we serve families. We are tethered to our clients well past the transaction. The transaction is just the tool that is the beginning of our long, faithful relationship with our tribe. No matter what industry you are in, if you come from a place of truly nurturing people, serving them at a high level, and staying in touch, you will see fruit. Speaking of fruit, as I mentioned earlier, I am a farmer's daughter. I understand the concept of planting, plowing, watering, spraying for weeds, and harvesting. This is a repetitive cycle and none of the steps can be skipped. We must plant, till, nurture, weed, water, and constantly nourish before the bountiful harvest comes, then repeat. This is true with our clients and our friends and family. We have to have bullet-proof systems, reminders, accountability measures set up so we don't falter.

We have learned so much about ourselves and about owning our own business, now we have this stirring to share it with others.

"Help others achieve their dreams and you will achieve yours." —Les Brown

I love this quote! I get so much more gratification from helping others self-discover, realize their potential, or feel empowered to take that leap of faith. When you combine purpose and passion, the profit comes, and you are blessed exponentially.

We sell houses, a lot of them. Sure, jumping up and down or doing a back handspring in sheer celebration with a "sold in one day" sign is fun! But what gets me out of bed every day is knowing I am going to be used in some way to make a bigger difference. I may be able to solve a problem, put out a fire, give someone peace of mind, or find a solution to a bleak situation, and take actionable steps to move forward in whatever their situation is. I can refer them to another expert who I know can help if I don't have the answers, even do some creative marketing online to quench my artsy side. The underlying reason I do all those things is to be a difference maker. We are in this to build relationships and serve people. I am so grateful real estate has been the vehicle that has allowed us to become debt free and start aggressively saving for retirement, but more importantly, I'm grateful to have an impact and for the opportunity to influence others in our community and industry.

One of the reasons I know we are being referred so frequently is we are building relationships and connecting with people on a deeper level than just superficial. Social media is a two-way street. For me, it is not just about being social, it is about peeling back layers. Sure, it is a mix of 80/20 rule. Eighty percent of what I post is entertaining, inspiring, educational, and twenty percent is business related or reminding people we do real estate in creative, out of the box ways.

One thing I have not posted a lot about is my daughter's battle with an eating disorder. Out of respect for her privacy, I have not posted about it in depth for many years. Eating disorders are a shameful, secret epidemic. Being such a huge part of our lives, it was hard not to share or ask for encouragement. She has since come to a place where she has opened up in order to raise awareness. An eating disorder, otherwise known in my house as ED, is a terrorist. ED (eating disorder) had taken over my daughter's mind and body, like an alien. ED has become the monster within. ED is an enemy who lies, steals, and destroys our daughter's identity and self-confidence. He was completely skewing her view of reality. This once joy-filled, energetic, happy, easy going, silly girl was replaced by an empty, hollow, dark, hurting, hopeless shell of a person. I felt like I lived with a total stranger. It affected the entire family to its core. When living with this disorder, they are so lifeless at times. I would need to help her put her feet on the floor just to face the day. The simplest of tasks seemed like a marathon. The eating disorder has disrupted and wrecked our lives for the last six years. Jordyn did not go to traditional high school, never attended a prom nor a formal graduation, and was in and out of treatment at some of the finest facilities in the country. Recently, my daughter finally began to post content regarding her eating disorder.

I was approached by someone at Life Church to write a blog on how we can educate and provide a support system from a mother's perspective. The families oftentimes are paralyzed by the change that happens in their children and the life-threatening risk. My goal in writing some content was to help parents first identify there is a cause for concern and second, to offer some lines of help. Like us, parents are not prepared or equipped to fix this disorder. The last time our daughter entered treatment was November 2019. It was so difficult as she was on track to start an intense outpatient elevated treatment plan to keep her out of going inpatient. Compounding the disorder being at its worst with a major trauma, is truly debilitating. When Jordyn was away at treatment, she had her twenty-first birthday. I had been feeling stirred to send her a video or do a Facebook live on her birthday. I wanted to actually sing her a song, not send a YouTube link, but for her to hear her mother's own voice filled with love and hope. I put it off and kept trying to talk myself out of doing it out of selfish fear of what others may think. I finally set a lit candle on top of my car and propped the camera against the candle. I just wanted Jordyn and anyone else to really let the lyrics resonate and move them, not focus on me in the video. Singing on Facebook makes me feel pretty vulnerable. I can perform in front of large crowds, but there is something about putting a video out there and never knowing what comments you will hear, good or bad. But.I knew I was supposed to post it. I also felt that not just Jordyn needed to hear this song about believing our identity is who God says we are. We allow negative thoughts and influences to decide the inadequacies in our hearts and minds are true. They are not. I know, I struggle with this daily and so many do.

MY MINI-ME, JORDYN AND I

THE FOCUS WAS ON THE LYRICS, NOT ME

I posted this:

I might as well be naked with how vulnerable I feel. I am in my garage in the dark.

This is me singing to not only my daughter, but anyone that needs to hear the words, "YOU ARE ENOUGH."

You see a candle burning instead of me singing because I want you to allow the lyrics to sink in. Our identity comes from Christ, not the world, not from a disease, but from God.

I pray this will minister to anyone that needs hope. I haven't formally warmed up my vocal chops for a year. If you hear a break in my voice, it isn't a mistake. This is from the depths of my soul, a mother's prayer, and cry for healing! By the way, I have wrestled with posting this and did it in one take. It is not about perfection; it is about where the heart is.

Being vulnerable with our struggles and battles helps others. How can we pray for you or your loved ones?

Happy Birthday Jordyn McPherson

Shortly after I posted the video, I walked away and left my phone in the other room. Soon, Troy came in and told me I just received a heart-wrenching message and I needed to read it. The friend told me he had just gone out into his garage with a plan to end his life. While scrolling through Facebook looking for some kind of a sign to spare his life, he heard my song. I can remember reading this message and tears welling up inside me. I was so grateful he did not end his life. We underestimate the power of God using us in what we consider small ways.

> Denise,
> Thank you for posting that video.
> I've struggled with depression for many years and today has been the hardest I've had in a while. As I'm sitting in my garage, chain smoking and planning on ending everything, I signed into Facebook to post my final goodbye. I'm scrolling and scrolling and trying to find something to live for. I came across your video and watched through teary eyes. Finally just closing my eyes and listening to the words. The words came from God but through your voice, I knew it wasn't over. I knew there were reasons to continue.
> I'm sharing this because I want you to know the impact you make, even on those that you may not expect to.
> Thank you.

This story is so powerful to me. For one, thinking to myself how many times I felt stirred to post this song and kept putting it off due to my own insecurities and vulnerabilities. We simply HAVE to get out of our own way and listen to the still small voice. I am so glad I was obedient and posted the song. God was just using me as a vehicle to breathe hope into a hopeless soul. We don't always know what the magnitude of stepping out of our comfort zone will be, but it is always worth it. I received another message the next morning from another friend who told me a similar story. She is a young, single, new mother, overwhelmed financially, and just was feeling hopeless. We all have to peel back and not be afraid to show ourselves. Posting great content that receives a lot of engagement is not success. Showing who you genuinely are connects you with others in a way you can't even imagine. The relatability for showing weaknesses or fears is astounding. People don't want perfection; they want raw transparency and relatability.

My challenge to you again is to get comfortable being uncomfortable. When we commit to owning those weaknesses, trials, failures, and deep struggles, they draw us closer to those who need hope and will open up to us because we are relatable.

Writing and expressing myself have often afforded me the permission to share on many stages and platforms. I never dreamt that I would be writing content to help parents of children with eating disorders. If you told me twenty years ago that I would have been given the opportunity to reach, influence, and impact others who are in desperate need of help, I would have laughed.

There are some major events in a person's life. The most precious and pivotal times are your engagement, marriage, pregnancies, deaths, promotions, graduations, etc. When you know you honestly have a relationship business, not just a referral business, there is such a shift. I have been asked to sing at the funerals of a client's parents and even weddings. We are invited to showers, cookouts, weddings, birthday parties, adoption ceremonies, dinners, or to just come catch up!

One of the most precious acts of love I can give others is to sing at their loved one's funeral. Being able to use my gift in this way is nothing short of incredible. One of my most fond memories was being in the balcony of this gorgeous Catholic church singing. When you open yourself up to serve and use your God-given gifts and talents, you will be used when and where you least expect it. When you are vulnerable with others, you give them an invitation to also peel back some layers.

Vulnerability creates a true connection which is a shared pain. There is something so profound knowing you are not alone, and we are all in this together.

As explained by Brene Brown, people with a strong sense of love and belonging believe that vulnerability is a necessity. They believe that within their vulnerabilities are the things that make them beautiful. And they're right. Vulnerability is key to connection because it is the courage to be open to another human.

Questions to ask yourself:

If I am transparent today, how can I help someone else?

What is my story? What message can I share with others through my journey?

What deep waters have I walked through that will help someone else not feel alone?

Have you gone through the tunnel, made it to the other side, and reached the light? You will inspire others by sharing what you have been able to overcome!

What is holding you back from doing it?

In my holding back, what am I robbing from someone else who needs to see hope and know others have made it through the darkness?

Chapter 16
When the Heart Leads

I have what you would call a disease to please. I have always had this deep desire to please others around me and make everyone comfortable and happy.

It is not a rare occasion for me to roll out a literal red carpet for our guests and gatherings. Our neighbors probably think someone famous is coming over when they see the red carpet down the long sidewalk up to our home. Our guests are famous to us, and we want friends, family, and clients to feel our deep adoration. When we have overnight guests, I love to put chocolates and a handwritten card on the bed expressing our gratitude for their company. In the morning, we have fresh coffee and a custom omelet made to order from our family chef, Troy.

"HOME ISN'T A PLACE; IT'S A FEELING; IT'S THE PEOPLE WHO MAKE YOU FEEL THAT YOU BELONG." -J.C. REED

WE GENUINELY CREATE A SPACE TO LAUGH, LET LOOSE AND HAVE FUN WITH OUR CLIENTS.

We had a clear vision in our branding from the beginning to give superior treatment. We want our clients to feel special, valued, adored, appreciated, and worthy of the red-carpet treatment. At all our events, we have a red carpet and a paid photographer that makes people feel special. We want our people to feel appreciated and celebrated. I absolutely love the quote, "I've learned that people will forget what you said, people will forget what you did, but people will never forget how you made them feel." Maya Angelou

I have learned from starting to work at an early age, no matter the profession, we are here to make a difference. Seek the opportunities to give now. You are never too young to start.

My initial intent to start working at the earliest age possible was for a selfish, vain reason. My Dad only paid me ten cents a day to cut the Futures Market section out of the Journal Tribune. That was not going to get me my designer wardrobe I thought was a must-have to support my social status. You see, I love fashion. Being fashionable costs money. My parents would not spring for the most expensive, designer jeans. They taught me at a young age, if you want to be extravagant, go work for it and pay for it yourself, so I started working at age 15. The phrase, "will work for food," was in my case, "will work for fashion status." I won the Best Dressed award at our senior assembly. I used to carry spare outfits in my backpack to school, as well as bright lipstick and blush. I have never wanted to be in someone else's box, even if it meant getting grounded. It was always a joke between my mom and I since I had to go to work to be able to express myself through attire.

I have always had a deep love for the elderly and spent a lot of time with all my grandparents. There was a very nice nursing home a few blocks from my childhood home. I applied there when I was a freshman in high school. Coincidentally, I had three great-grandparents who were in the assisted living section of this nursing home facility. I had a passion for being able to provide comfort and peace of mind for family members leaving the total care and well-being of their loved ones to people like me. It was the hardest work I have ever done. It was physically taxing and emotionally exhausting. I was lifting, turning, feeding, changing bedpans, bed pads, showering, but most of all, loving these patients. As a 15-year-old, this was a huge responsibility that I took very seriously. I was able to build relationships with the patients and their families. I saw so much death, loss, and hurt in those halls. These patients were more than a room number or patient on a roster. I was caring for someone's mother, sister, grandmother, daughter, friend, father, grandfather, son, brother. When a family knew the days I worked, they would tell me they knew their loved ones would be spoiled and cared for in a special way. One of the moments I will never forget was being bedside with a patient who was dying. Her name was Edna Elsenrath. She had no family there, and me and a co-worker vowed to not leave her alone. We stayed after our shift was over knowing she had merely hours to live. The last words she said to us were a poem she recited by Frank Loesser. She expressed how grateful she was that we loved her and that she loved us.

I will never forget that moment, but more than anything, I will remember how full my heart was knowing, at 99 years old, she had peace and joy in her last moments on this earth. She felt loved, cared for, and cherished until the end. I went to her funeral and spoke to one of her kids who lived out of state. I was able to share stories of how she spoke so fondly about memories of her children growing up and how proud she was of all of them. She hugged me for a long time, and when we parted ways, she said, "You are an angel. Thank you for loving my mom and making her last days more joyous and bearable." I thought in my self-centered teenage mind that I was the one making such a difference and impact for these patients and families. Instead, I discovered I was the one who was rewarded and my cup truly runneth over serving others. I grew to understand the importance of intentionally focusing on how we make people feel. I craved more of that feeling of making a difference.

Another early experience with serving people was waiting tables. I had always played waitress when our family would have fifty-plus guests at gatherings. One of my gifts, you could say, is being very hospitable. There has always been something inside me that has a desire to serve others. I was so good at being anticipatory. My Grandfather Shepherd was a huge influence in my life. He always taught me to be one step ahead in anything I pursued. I loved to anticipate when the patron needed a refill, a new basket of chips, extra napkins, or a coloring book for the kids. I found I could create an uninterrupted dining experience if I always was one step ahead of their needs. I did very well waiting on tables in college and made good money. The best compliment working the food industry is when your patrons request you by name to serve them and then become regulars.

I have an amazing story about building a relationship with customers, no matter how small you feel like your job or impact is on the world. I got to know this lovely older couple. We had conversations about my preparations for my upcoming wedding. They kept telling me their granddaughter had an extravagant wedding dress that did not get used, it was in perfect, mint condition. They were adamant about me trying on this dress. I felt awkward at first, but they finally wore me down, and I agreed to come try the dress on. I went to their home and fell in love with this Princess Diana-caliber designer dress with a train that felt like it went on for the length of the sanctuary. It had lace, intricate beading, fit me like a glove, but most of all I remember how I felt when I saw myself in the mirror for the first time. I felt unrecognizable to myself. I could hardly see myself from the welling of tears. I immediately said, "Yes to the dress!" It was a magical moment and I ended up renting it from them for $100, an amazing price to wear a dress I would have never been able to afford. They reluctantly took the $100, but my mother would not let them refuse it. My parents were frugal, and they were not going to be able to spend thousands on a dress like this. I will never forget the joy when we were all standing in their living room crying happy tears because they knew this dress was making a dream come true. I truly felt like a princess. They were so blessed and rewarded by me wearing this dress. It was such a special anchoring moment in my life.

My mom was incredible at leaving people feeling immensely welcomed, loved, and cherished. She had a contagious warmth around her that was magnetizing. I am so grateful she passed this trait down to me. It is a great legacy and responsibility to spread love and seek to make deposits in people's lives, rather than being a consumer. It is a huge part of my emotional make-up, and for that I am grateful. I carry her heart in mine to this day, even after her passing nearly twenty years ago.

How about doing something that may put you out of your comfort zone? One of my childhood best friends, Heidi, had recently had to put her dad, Bobby, into a rehabilitative assisted living after numerous falls at home. Bobby was really struggling, losing his independence, and not being able to drive and go around town being the social butterfly that he is. I call Heidi, Julie, and me The Three Amigos. We have been thick as thieves for decades. We are partners in crime, we have been there for one another through all the stages of life. We have grown up together, had babies together, mourned losing parents, and been there to celebrate wins or hold one another up when we feel defeated. We can share gut giggles or feel each other's pain as if it were our own. I have been held up and carried more times than I can count during the lows and grit of my life by these two.

I concocted the idea of me bringing tutus and some cute eclectic headbands and meeting at the nursing home facility to do a cheer up visit for our sweet Bobby. Bobby was suffering from Alzheimer's, and on any given day you did not know what mental state he would be in where his memory was concerned, which causes fear, confusion, and restlessness. The girls were hesitant, thinking I was nuts, but as always, they went along with the idea after a few minutes of negotiating and coaxing them into it. We all put our garb on and walked through the facility. We turned heads, but most of all we gave these folks, cooped up in this center after major health issues and rehab journeys, a smile! And not the polite, no-teeth grin, but an ear to ear, light up your life SMILE! We were disrupting their day with joy. Heidi had been exhausted from running back and forth with a two-hour commute home making sure her dad felt cared for even with the distance. Dealing with dementia was draining for all, it was truly heartbreaking to witness the decline. I know Heidi and Julie can tell you spreading this joy far outweighed their level of discomfort from being grown women dressing up in a tutu! When we reached Bobby's room, he lit up like a Christmas tree. He truly was delighted and happy. He proceeded to parade us around and introduce us to all the staff in the facility. He was so proud and excited about our visit! You see, that is what it is all about, how we make people feel. I know when we left, the feeling of pure reward was ours. We went in to bless the patients and boost morale. We left with our own cups full and Heidi having a much-needed recharge.

What do you do that makes a difference?

I call them WOO moments! We do our best to create them whenever we can. Even the smallest efforts sometimes make the biggest difference. The opportunities are there in both personal and professional life. As you go through your day, look around you. There are openings for us to show love, extend encouragement, and possibly be the only positive interaction someone receives that day. Think about that! Be the reason someone smiles today and EVERYDAY! Are you tracking with me? I challenge you to listen to that small voice that guides and prompts us to take action, no matter how big or small.

No matter what your industry is or what job title you have, open your ears, eyes, and heart to give as you go daily. We are all given liberty to seek and be hyper aware of needs around us. Sometimes it is no more than a pay-it-forward Starbucks order. It can be an encouraging compliment, a listening ear, even helping someone load their groceries.

"In all things I have shown you that by working hard in this way we must help the weak and remember the words of the Lord Jesus, how he himself said, 'It is more blessed to give than to receive.'"

(English Standard Version Bible, 2001 Acts 20:35)

HEIDI AND HER DAD, BOBBY

THE THREE AMIGOS: HEIDI, JULIE AND I

There is no secret sauce. You can have creativity around your genuine personality, but it boils down to loving and serving people. In my marketplace, it is saturated. I feel like everywhere I turn, someone I know is a realtor or wants to get their license. My Facebook messages are inundated with people asking how they can do what I do. I feel like we do such a good job at making it look so fun, it makes everyone want to join in! I knew from doing my own real estate transactions, there were incredible realtors and ones only out for the almighty buck. I was a victim of that situation and had to release a local power couple in my own past real estate selling experience.

If you compare your customer experiences with many different places you frequent, you definitely are drawn to the companies that have a story and make you feel warm, appreciated, and valued.

I had this fire inside me when I was truly given an opportunity to show my love for people. I wanted to serve "like I was chosen." This phrase is repeated throughout this book because it is my mission to walk in this mindset daily. I knew we wanted to build a system to serve where nothing fell through the cracks, and we would create a bullet proof process for our clients.

In my industry, our clients buy/sell homes every five to seven years. This process is new or completely blurry to them, and they need to trust us to be the designated navigator. In our checklists, we always ask ourselves, "What is the next step?" We don't want clients to EVER have to ask, "What is next?" The feeling of uncertainty is frightening to most people and causes great stress. We want to give them the peace of mind that we are leading them and have everything down to the last detail handled.

Seek opportunities outside of yourself to extend joy, relief, and live out your why through helping others. Lending yourself to making someone else's day is so much more gratifying than meeting any quota. Sometimes it is about getting out of your own way and your comfort zone. Other times, it is about you helping to lead others and walking with them outside of their comfort zones. Magical things happen when the heart leads and we listen to the needs of others, whether spoken or unspoken.

When you start doing this in your personal life, it filters into your professional life as well. Make it a habit to take a Blessing Break every day! Do some act of kindness, big or small, to impact the life of someone else. I promise this will make your day so much richer and fulfilling!

Chapter 17
She Wears Many Hats

As realtors, we all wear many hats. I am often a listener, counselor, troubleshooter, firefighter, confidante, and definitely a director of more than just a transaction. You see, I have a few job descriptions. I really hate the phrase *job description* though. I like *privilege description* much better. At the time of this writing, we are in the midst of a global pandemic. The unemployment rate went from a historic low of five percent to thirteen percent. It is a privilege to have work. The things I do for people are my greater calling. We meet people where they are and take them arm in arm. We celebrate BIG and we are never afraid to get on our knees and pray with them. Being used in this way makes me absolutely love what we are blessed to do. My dad farmed for fifty years before retiring a couple of years ago. After high school, he went to earn his agriculture degree and stepped right back into the family business. He told me that he does not feel like he works. Presently, he has retired and leased out his land, but he still goes to the farm every single day. He helps out, volunteers his time, and spends quality moments, after fifty years on the job, because he truly loves farming. The old saying that if you find something you love, you never have to work a day in your life is not a cliche in my world. I watched my dad get up at 6 am with a fire in his belly every single day. He was respected in his industry and recognized for being a smart risk taker, leading him to be one of the most innovative in his field. He received highly esteemed awards and is my inspiration for my work ethic. Another saying rings true to me, "Be the hardest worker in the room." I saw him love not only farming, but that what he loved gave so much back to him in return.

One of the most bittersweet and precious moments in my entire life was witnessing my grandmother, while on her deathbed, spending an afternoon with her best friend of many decades. I grew up spending a lot of time with my grandparents. My Grandma Patti's best friend was Ina Ellington. They had a bridge club that met every week, and I was a common fixture playing waitress, as usual. Ina is an absolute spitfire and a barrel of laughs. She was one of the most treasured humans to our family. My grandpa had passed after sixty-seven years of marriage, and Ina was so incredibly special to Grandma Patti. Ina lives independently about an hour away from the nursing home where my grandmother was. She should not be driving anywhere outside the local area near her home. She snuck out and drove forty-five minutes, at age ninety, making the journey to be with my grandma in her last hours. When Ina entered the room and their eyes met, my grandmother beamed with some of the purist joy I have ever witnessed. I saw tears stream down their faces and their giggles echoed, filling the nursing home halls with pure joy. I listened to them reminisce. To hear them, you would not have known how weak grandma actually was, or that it was almost time for her to leave earth behind. She was energized, and the two told stories and filled in each other's sentences and cackled about details one or the other forgot. These two had such genuine love and care for one another. They had truly done life together and were so grateful for this time together. I sat there nearly paralyzed from emotions running wild. I could not even see because I had so many tears well up. I could hardly even swallow from attempting to not break out in a full ugly cry. Moments like these force us to step back and shift all perspectives.

We all need to have reflective moments where we reevaluate what is important. I know that this is a marketing book. This story has nothing to do with real estate. It hopefully does, however, fill your heart with hope. We all should treasure the time we have. Tomorrow is not guaranteed. If you think something, say it. Don't hold anything back. Stories are so powerful and live on through each and every one of us. I was blessed enough to be raised by incredible storytellers. For years, I felt like my book was finished and I had no story worth telling. Today, I know I have a story, and the imperfections make it that much more impactful and beautiful.

GRANDMA AND INA

At the end of the day, we are brought into a client's world in close quarters. We are in their dance space. There are realtors in our profession only out for the almighty dollar. For you to be successful in this field, you can't just be a hard worker. You have to be business-minded, have passion, stamina, and a genuine love and care for others. People are literally putting their largest investments in our hands. It is our ethical responsibility to handle each and every detail and step with the utmost care. As mentioned earlier, you truly realize when you are asked to sing at clients' parents' funerals, attend birthday parties, showers, and sporting events, you have a relationship-centric referral business.

THE GREATEST HONOR IS BEING ASKED
TO SING AT A FUNERAL

SOMETIMES
you will
NEVER KNOW
the value
of a MOMENT
until it becomes
a MEMORY.
-Dr. Seuss-

DR SEUSS QUOTE

You are in this for the long game. Deliver jackpot service. Have you ever had that client you were able to help through every detail, along every step of the way? You knew that you had not only a client, but an ambassador for you for life.

What are you NOT doing that you can do to create this experience? It does not mean the transaction is without stress or hiccups. It is all in how you react and pace the pitfalls. You are the aspirin and the stabilizing force, hell or high water, you are there to protect and serve their interests.

What can you add to your menu of services that can lead to this jackpot service mentality? If all our clients felt they had hit the jackpot by choosing us, it could be life changing.

If you are struggling to add some WOO factors in your business, make a list of pain points.

What complaints or frustrations have others expressed that you can attribute to a hard-to-please mentality?

When you get hired after another realtor could not get the job done, what were the reasons the client gave for dissatisfaction? Complaints and failures are a gift. It is a sign to reverse engineer your journey from top to bottom.

When we sit down with clients who have fired or released a prior agent, we dive deeper. That does not mean we are there to jump in and talk trash on fellow agents. We are there to solve their problems, not fixate on another's poor performance. The top complaints we have heard over the years are as follows:

Poor Communication (Hands down the number one complaint).

Failure to educate on the process, verbiage, contracts.

Insufficient marketing efforts.

Unprofessionalism.

Pathetic negotiation skills.

Sellers get handed off to assistant or another random agent.

Tardy.

Fails to follow-through.

Voicemail too full.

Hired a friend/family member that was inexperienced and not well-versed with legal docs, negotiating, or market.

One of the things we implemented early on is a very tailored information email campaign system that is automatic during each transaction. We never ever want a client to wonder what is happening next. We do this every single day. Some of your clients have never bought or sold, or it has been years since they've gone through this process. This is the biggest deal in their life, whether a $10,000 investment home or a $1.8 million luxury home fit for an NBA star.

My grandfather taught me early on that if you are not ten minutes early, you are late. Coincidentally, I get lost everywhere I go. This is ironic for a realtor to be directionally challenged. I was taught a man's time is such a valuable commodity, you don't ever take it for granted. I have lived by this. My husband and I get into squabbles because he waits until ten minutes before we need to leave to even start getting ready. There is a country song, "Waitin' on a Woman." In my case, it is "Waitin' on a Man." Due to this lifelong habit, I have to always be prepared and punctual.

Clean your voicemail out. When I hear a message that a mailbox is full, this tells me that they do not diligently check their messages and tend to them, so they likely won't receive my message. It does not project the image that this person is professional and keeps up with their business efficiently.

We used to be guilty of taking our own real estate photos. We had a photography business at one point and loved it. My specialty is natural light and taking pictures of humans and animals. Taking indoor photography is a different story. Something we were trying to do to save money became so time consuming and ended up costing us money. We now hire a fantastic company that makes our listings sell faster due to the quality of images. The vast majority of all buyers start online before they even set up a showing. That's why having cutting edge real estate marketing is imperative for getting clients in the door.

These are just a few easy things we focus on that make a difference in how our image is projected from day one.

Chapter 18
Hitting the Jackpot

The beautiful recipe of our business model is first of all using bullet-proof systems, then marrying many gifts and strengths and tethering them all together so they just naturally flow. One thing we strive to do is fulfill our promises. We always want to be one step ahead of our clients. Our ultimate goal is to serve in a very anticipatory fashion. Systems help allow us to flourish in this area. Even if your client has bought and sold before and is seasoned in this process, nothing is more frustrating than wondering what is next. We always want to let the client know the next steps so they can be prepared and aware each step of the way.

In our business it is imperative to also recognize our weaknesses and delegate those out. It is really easy to have a blind spot when evaluating your own organization. We are able to capture attention and establish branding and name recognition through a variety of power-packed ways. Our goal is to use many different methods to stay top of mind! In our case we use a very strategic, organic social marketing approach. Our approach is a balanced blend of our hobbies, our private life, our business, design trends, our TV appearances, media exposures, and most importantly, showing the stories of our treasured customers.

It is my hope that what you have read in this book sparks something in you to move into uncharted territory and ramp up your existing game or completely reverse engineer it altogether. Take it from a small-town girl who delayed her dream calling for two decades before finally being led to opportunities and accomplishments she'd never thought were even in the realm of possibility. It is never too late to reinvent, recharge, or even restart from scratch.

We seek to find opportunities to go above and beyond and hopefully leave a lasting imprint while we build a rich and meaningful relationship with our clients. One extra touch is we use props for our photo shoots and closings. One of my all-time favorites was this one! We sold their home in one day and made happy sellers out of them. Good is the biggest enemy to great. We don't just want to give good customer service; we want to give a jackpot customer service experience.

Our intention is that every client feels lucky and blessed, like they have hit the jackpot by having us on their side in their real estate transactions. These are big shoes to fill but wooing others and making people feel cared and advocated for is truly what it is all about!

The clients in the photo on the next page were elated with our service and results. Shawn even asked to keep the hat as a memento of this celebratory milestone!

HITTING THE JACKPOT

Chapter 19
Give them a reason to RAVE!
(Growing Influence through Reviews)

What do other people say about you?

What are you known for?

What service do you provide that no one else does?

It does not matter how many times you say how amazing you are or playfully pose holding the number one finger symbol up. If others do not rave about you, spread the good word about you, and ultimately do your marketing for you, it just is not as effective. From the beginning of starting your real estate business, make this a priority! With the statistics showing that people are doing all things in life on the internet more now, we must show up there. Before I purchase anything, even a cheap blouse on Amazon, I read the reviews. I see people post positives and negatives about the arrival, return policies, the sizing, the quality, and even photos of consumers wearing the product. This gives me peace and buying confidence to hit "add to cart."

It is like pulling teeth sometimes to get people to do a review. Time is valuable and so we must give the level of service that will cause people to want to help you grow your business. It takes extra time that they may not have, so this is also your opportunity to exhibit a sense of gratitude. Offering incentives like a $5 Starbucks card, etc., is a great tool to thank people for taking the time. (Please check with your state regulations on what you are allowed to do in your city.) It also teaches them how important it is to you that they refer you to others because you will serve them well. In general, people like to help others.

We start communicating the importance for reviews at the beginning of the transaction when real estate is top of mind and top of their conversations. You will learn which clients love the limelight and they will be more apt to give you a video testimonial for the icing on the cake. Videos are life! You statistically get more views on a video than a text review showing five stars. Consumers want to hear their opinion of you out of the horse's mouth. We have review links we send, then we ask for a review personally, and have implemented a follow-up system to get the review! We have links for our Facebook business page, Yelp, Google, realtor.com, and Zillow. When I left my chiropractor's office after my first visit, I received a text message with three links to give reviews. I wrote a wonderful review and copy-pasted it in all three places, so I was able to leave three reviews for this company in a matter of minutes. It was easy, and they were so appreciative of my effort.

Here are some examples of treasured reviews our clients happily submitted:

They are the kindest realtors you will find, so much so they have become personal family friends! They helped my parents sell their beloved home and downsize. My parents were guided smoothly through the whole process. There was never a doubt that Troy and Denise knew each step to take and in the proper order. It gave my folks much peace in the buying and selling process. —Kim Cotter

Troy and Denise are the best team to work with hands down. They sold our house in less than two weeks and stayed by our side every step of the way as we bought our dream house, which was also a short sale. And trust me, short sales get crazy!! I would not have made it through the process without both of them. They are both so honest, up front, and treat you like their only client.

We had such a great experience with them when selling and buying last year, we used them again this year to help sell my father-in-law's house when he passed away. They sold his house in four days! They assist you every step of the way and are so attentive. And you won't beat their energy level and advertising skills! THANK YOU BOTH FOR ALL YOU HAVE DONE FOR US!! —Ashley Santoro

The Schroder Team helped me sell my house in just five short days a few years ago!! Honestly, they treated me like royalty and did everything in their power to make the process go smoothly and successfully. I was impressed at how they were always available to talk and communicated very promptly during the entire process. Keep selling and smiling! You all are the best! —Brittany Tolman

Troy and Denise have sold two properties for myself and my family. Both experiences resulted in an above asking price within one day of listing the property. I have also purchased two homes with them. Because of their knowledge, I paid a fair price and eventually sold the first one three years later for $15,000 dollars more than what I bought it for. If you listen and follow their recommendations, you will come out on top whether you are buying or selling your home. —Lori White

Reviews are a vital tool in your business. They give you credibility with anyone wishing to interview you to help with a real estate need. Gathering reviews is much like building your database. It is a daily task that should be prioritized. I cannot tell you how many referrals come from out-of-state agents or local consumers who said they scoured the internet for top agents and read every word of our reviews. They are powerful!

When posting reviews, I lead with a bit of text that says, "This is why we love doing what we do." People connect with the "why" more than the "who" or "what." Drawing people in with the breadth of these stories of happy, inspired, and grateful clients is what it is all about.

More than anything, I love to have a video testimonial review rather than a text. I am eternally grateful for both, but videos are so much more powerful than text any day! The emotions and expressions are amplified, and the heartstrings pull when connected with someone's journey! Testimonials are one of the most powerful drivers of purchasing behavior. We regularly have testimonial videos produced to tell a story as well as creating posts of single testimonial videos. How powerful it is to be able to send a string of video testimonials to a new customer who has never met you in order to express the message that you will serve them well.

The next best thing to having my best friend rave to me about a realtor is a powerful, organic video testimonial!

Reviews should be prioritized right along with your database! Communicating to your client how this is so helpful and valuable to your business is key. Don't be shy about expressing how critical and essential it is to your credibility and growth. Don't just ask for a review. Make sure you tell your customer the WHY! When other people feel they can make a difference, it is much more motivating and compelling for them to do an act of service for you. Give the level of service that will motivate people to want to help your business.

I recently listened to a webinar with the Anderson-Hicks team from Keller Williams. As a team, from the ground up they all communicate the unified message that the common goal is to deliver a promise. The "Promise" is simple, but intentional from every spoke of their company. They will provide an experience that you could not imagine being any better and seek a referral by the end of the escrow period. If the client does not provide a referral, it leaves the team wondering what they did wrong and they will actively seek to find out for growth purposes. Reviews and referrals are the very nucleus of the business. Reviews also reveal a client's journey and story, which I absolutely love!

The greatest verbal review we have ever received was from a client who sold multiple properties at a time with us. She was going through a lot of life change and relied heavily on us to help her navigate through the processes. She told us at closing that she knew we had tons of clients we were actively serving. However, she said we made her feel like she was our ONLY client. These were the most beautiful words strung together. This is magic if we can make clients feel there is no silly question, no unimportant concern, or small detail that does not matter to us as much as it does to them. This goes for our personal lives as well. Being attentive, present, proactive, anticipatory, and empathetic is so important to earning trust and making your people feel cared and advocated for immensely.

Are you asking for reviews?

Are you giving the service that evokes others to share and refer to you?

What is your system and follow-through to build reviews?

Tips:

Ask for reviews while momentum is high! When you sell the home for top dollar or win multiple offers, this is a great time to get a powerful review.

Take the pressure off people. Not everyone is a writer. Remind your customers those one or two sentences is awesome and greatly appreciated!

Chapter 20
Pay it Forward

You want a natural high? Show gratitude to another human being, just because. The feeling of being appreciated is better than a new pair of shoes, and that is saying a lot coming from me!

I love doing gratitude videos. We used to try to cram them all in November and now we do one a day to our past clients and sphere of influence. It is so quick and easy to do a thirty-second video just saying you are thinking about them, hoping they are well, and thanking them for being a part of your tribe and support system.

To take things another step further, we have had so much fun backtracking and reminiscing on what is called the great retrace, a strategy for gaining those all-important reviews. I learned about the retrace from a friend and amazing author, Michael Maher. He wrote an incredible book called *The Seven Levels of Communication*. We have implemented so many things into our business, I highly recommend his book. He comes from such a sincere place of generosity and contribution.

Angel has referred us to families who have then bought and sold through us multiple times as well. There were referrals stemming off from each client referred, if I were to go deeper.

RETRACE
ANGEL MYERS

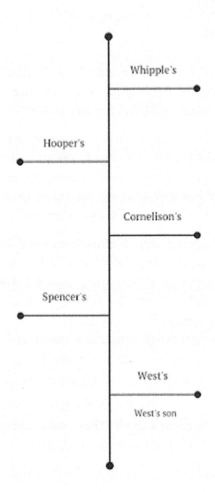

Whipple's

Hooper's

Cornelison's

Spencer's

West's

West's son

RETRACE REFERRAL CHART

Troy and I attended a coaching skills camp with our brokerage on Coronado Island in California. We got to be a part of something so incredible. The staff at the hotel worked tirelessly to keep our conference room clean, stocked with drinks and snacks, and keep our restrooms tidy, and did it all with a million-dollar smile. Our instructor, Diana Kokoska, said that she needed our help with something she does at every event she teaches at. She arranged with the hotel manager to have the entire staff walk through in single file across our stage. They had no idea what was going on. From the moment the first staff team member walked through the door, we were on our feet, screaming and chanting at the top of our lungs! To see the utter surprise and shock on their faces with such humble appreciation was not easy to describe. There were many of the hundreds in the room with tears running down our cheeks. As they left the conference room, we lined up to high-five them. I could barely see I was crying so hard. As we all have done at one time or another, we have felt we were stuck in a thankless j-o-b. I felt like that for years and it struck such a chord with me that day. These folks work so hard to serve others, are not paid that well, and are probably rarely thanked, much less given a standing ovation, ten-minute roar session with 300 beaming faces smiling at them with sheer joy. To be able to give another human being an experience like that is one I will never forget! Jesse Cole talks about high-five lines from the baseball players and staff when fans enter and leave the building. How cool is that? Talk about bringing the energy up in a supreme way!

I sang the national anthem at our awards show for Keller Williams. I often sing at the opening of the ceremony. The last time I sang acapella, and the entire crowd sprang to their feet to give me a standing ovation. That feeling is indescribable and left me completely euphoric. I walked around on cloud nine for hours after that experience. It was so much more gratifying than a plaque for our yearly production. What if we could make people around us feel so extremely appreciated and valued? Look at every opportunity to make a lasting impression and imprint on someone's life.

"I THINK EVERYONE IN LIFE SHOULD EXPERIENCE A STANDING OVATION AT LEAST ONCE IN THEIR LIVES. - RJ'S PALACIO WONDER

I am currently reading *The Thank You Project: Cultivating Happiness One Letter at a Time*. I am committed to writing a thank you note every single day for this entire year.

"Feeling gratitude and not expressing it is like wrapping a present and not giving it."

—William Arthur Ward

I am committing this year to writing a thank you note every single day to show gratitude to those who have made an impact on my life.

I recently had a dear friend tragically pass in his early thirties. I wrote a letter thanking and expressing my adoration for Brad to his parents and late wife. I shared in detail how he impacted my life in a monumental way. The response I received beyond filled my cup. I wrote the letter to bless them however, I felt more blessed than I could ever measure.

What are ways you can start to show appreciation and gratitude in small ways daily?

Tip: Ask each and every client their favorite things. Keep them on file and use them as a guide to sprinkle personal things throughout the year at random times.

Do you tell others how much you appreciate them?

Who can you thank today? It truly takes only a few seconds to send a text, or better yet, write a hand-written card.

Who is adding value to your life and why are you grateful?

Suggested Books:

Thank and Grow Rich: A 30-Day Experiment in Shameless Gratitude and Unabashed Joy

The Thank-You Project: Cultivating Happiness One Letter of Gratitude at a Time.

Chapter 21
Pop-Bys

This is one thing I struggled with at first. Lucky for me, my husband used to be a FedEx guy. I have a couple of confessions for you. I am not only a terrible driver, but I can't find my way out of a paper sack. Troy has always been the type of guy who can distinctly remember your address or at least the location of your house or workplace if he's ever been there before. Recalling where everyone lives and works is a gift. He is THAT guy who just stops by unannounced. I, on the other hand, do not like it when someone drops by my house. I always want my house to be picked up and to look perfect. The last thing I personally want is a spontaneous visit if my house is a mess and I don't have a bra on. So, we have modified the pop-by a bit. We want to be conscientious of not being a pest or making someone feel uncomfortable if they don't like last minute drop ins. Knowing each client well will help you to gauge pop-bys. We give the people thirty minutes to an hour's notice. If they are home and give us the green light to stop by, great. If they do not respond, we leave a treat on their porch. Have we mentioned our love of the Ring doorbell? We can give them a video message to make it more personal or even do the quick dance n' dash we are famous for! We have been known to whip and nay-nay on many porches. Our friends and clients tag us and post the videos online and it is wonderful exposure! It is amazing to have your clients post their Ring doorbell video of your dance n' dash performances. It truly does stop the scroll and it is something that people don't soon forget.

What are you doing that no one else does?

We keep cool trinket items in the car. We have coffee mugs, tumblers, cute coasters, wine, spare gifts, and miscellaneous things. This comes in handy when you have taken notes or had your clients fill out a questionnaire on their favorite things! Knowing their favorite candy bar or special made-to-order Starbucks coffee or Sonic drink makes it even more thoughtful.

It is the thought that counts on steroids if your little inexpensive item you drop off is tailored to something you learned they love. If you picked up a 1000 Grand bar because you know it is Susie's favorite candy, you are winning! Knowing you remembered that small detail and walked it up to the door to deliver versus drop shipping, is so powerful.

When you grow your business and database to a certain number, it is really hard to do pop bys. However, don't be discouraged. You can do contests and giveaways and bring the clients to you! You can do a pie giveaway, or reverse prospecting! We post on social media and blast out to our database that we are giving away three fire pits, for example. You can be entered into the drawing if you leave a review. Each place you submit a review about our services gives you a small gift card. Always check your regulations in your area before having contests or giveaways.

This year, we are having apple cider and mini pumpkin Bundt cakes at our house. We will invite our top fifty to swing by to take a tour of our new home. At this time, we will give them our Christmas gift. That is one less delivery we have to do. We also get quality, face-to-face time with our sphere.

The latest piece we have added to our touches this year is our relationship with Client Giant. Can you imagine what your business would look like if your client knew how much you cared?

Their slogan is, "If your business is client-based, your future relies on your past. We've got you covered."

Client Giant offers different packages and tiers. We chose to have a gift sent to our clients once a quarter. It is sent, packaged beautifully with a note from us. Their branding is not on the package. Client Giant wants your clients to feel an organic, personal touch. I have often thought about creating a subscription-type gift cycle in our systems. This proves to be very time consuming. I get easily caught up in creativity and it diverts my attention from money generating efforts. If you have a larger staff, delegate this task out. I do not have a runner on staff for deliveries. If we take something to our client's door, we prefer to go ourselves. It is so much more personal. I also don't want to miss the opportunity to visit, leave a message, and sometimes do a fun dance on their Ring doorbell systems. We are on our first quarter, and I am optimistic we will have a good response. It also gives us a reason to reach out when we check in to see if they indeed received our gift and if they are enjoying it. We are not asking for anything in return in any of the verbiage on our message in the card with the gift. It is all about THEM.

When you do personal pop-bys, spread them out over a couple of months if needed so you are not overwhelmed!

If you are stumped or don't have a creative bone in your body, never fear. Google has you covered. Google pop-by ideas for client gifts. There are oodles of clever economical ways to express love and appreciation.

Chapter 22
It is About THEM, not me!

Client Appreciation events are my jam! Many realtors, especially those just starting out, can't imagine having the budget to put an event together, much less fund it. The fantastic thing about it is, depending on your budget, you can be creative with your events! I am frugal so stick with me and I will show you some innovative examples of how to get your party on! I have spent over $7,000 on an event and as little as $500 and my time.

One of my all-time favorite events was also one of the cheapest. I love setting up a mini photo session for our clients! Our most popular time has been in October right before it gets cold here in Oklahoma. I have a vintage couch and some holiday pillows, props, etc. You can tailor the session to just a family photo if the client does not prefer a holiday theme. I send out a newsletter, create a Facebook event, set up a Sly-broadcast call and mass text message giving instructions to reserve their spots. I use a simple Google form where the clients can easily input their information in the time slot they prefer, add their email address and cell phone for an easy reminder, and for delivery of the digital photos. We offer five FREE digital photos that I email to the client after editing is complete. We used to have a photography business, so it is something I am passionate about, and I enjoy connecting with our clients in this way. It gives me a creative outlet. I shoot in outdoor, natural light so editing is a breeze!

You can hire a photographer and it is very reasonable if you pay them hourly. We have hired out before, versus me shooting the photos, and the photographer even provided the vintage couch! The photographer collected their email addresses/cell number and delivered the photos. She even got some future photo sessions with many of our families.

A few days before our last photo session, I got a call from a client's boyfriend. He asked if I could help him pull off an impromptu, surprise proposal during their family shoot. He thought it was the perfect moment that Sam would not expect. I was so excited to be a part of this. I used to shoot engagements and weddings and I am a sap for all things love. I told him I would have a couple of props for the pics after he proposed. I personalized a heart chalkboard and wrote "She said YES!" for her daughter to hold in the pictures of the three of them. When my mom married my dad, I was five. This moment was very nostalgic for me. I could barely see through the lens to get the shots. This made my month! Our profession can be very fast-paced and stressful. Moments like this are why I do what I do. When you have amazing relationships with your clients, they invite you along to be an active part of their story and journey, well beyond the closing.

BRANDIE, MABLE AND LUCCA CELEBRATING LUCCA'S FIRST BIRTHDAY

People love their furry kids so much! I am that girl who is always up for a challenge. I have photographed newborns and thought that was incredibly complex. Photographing pets can feel more like you are in a circus of sorts. However, these are a blast to do. My last one was for a client when her pup was turning one! We did a celebratory session with both dogs and Brandie, their owner.

NEXT STOP...THE CHAPEL: SAM'S SURPRISE ENGAGEMENT

Holiday Events– You can very easily host a "Pictures with Santa" or "Pictures with The Easter Bunny" for a client appreciation event. These are very inexpensive and an easy way for you to market your business, and at the same time solve a problem that many families face. No one wants to stand in line for two hours waiting for a five-second picture with Santa, but they do want the picture for memories. You can do this in your office and totally sponsor the entire event. Remember that the lines are super long at the malls and most parents just want the pictures, so this is an easy way to get in front of them and brand yourself to remind people what you do for a living.

Last year I stood in line with my niece for almost three hours to get a picture with Santa. I was miserable. This is a parent's pain point in the mission to get that traditional Santa or Easter Bunny money-shot that goes in the annual photo album.

Plan a food truck party. Many builders use this idea at their brokers' open events. It is awesome because people eat outside and are not tracking food and crumbs throughout the house. We have a local food truck rally that is so fun. We get to go to one place and taste test several types of food. Once you have chosen your featured food truck, send out invites and announcements, create an event on Facebook, call, text, and email your clients to get the most participation from your efforts. Have a personalized display board about what the free meal package includes. You can hand out tickets to your people if other public patrons are around who you are not providing a meal for. You can also do a breakfast brunch with a coffee cart, pancake party theme, and serve mimosas if you would like. A money saving tip is do this for lunch, not dinner. Adding an option of an alcoholic drink can add up quickly.

On certain occasions, we celebrate BIG with our clients. We have two larger parties a year. We literally roll out the red carpet for our people! Every event is focused on how we make our clients feel. From the moment they step out of the car, we want them to feel they are the focal point. Red carpet is a staple at all our events, as well as hiring our very own paparazzi to capture moments. We provide our guests with a professional photo and a reason to dress up and paint the town red! We have a branded vinyl backdrop we spent a couple hundred bucks on, but we use it regularly, so it has paid for itself. Our guests are encouraged to use our hashtag to post on their timelines. Most of our guests love having a professional shot of themselves, so they actually make it their profile picture. Our branding on the backdrop of the photo is then circulating for mass exposure.

IT IS NOT A PARTY WITHOUT PROPS

MY BLACKWELL TRIBE

GIVE THEM THE PHOTO SHOOT OF THEIR DREAMS

GIRLS JUST WANNA HAVE FUN

THE MONEY SHOT OF THE NIGHT

FUN WITH PROPS, KIM AND CAROL

Here are some other ideas to consider for wooing your clients.

Baseball Game Night Out—If you want to give a great family night out, this is your ticket! Call your ballpark and ask about group/bulk rates and see if they can offer a special for a hotdog and a drink.

You can also have a viewing party. Even if you hate football, the Super Bowl is a gift. You can have a viewing party, even at your home if it will accommodate. Remember, you don't have to invite your entire sphere of influence to everything. You are going to want to have smaller, more intimate parties where you can truly visit and connect more than working a room when there are 300 clients all wanting to talk to you. When we have had our HGTV watch parties, it has felt similar to a wedding. We are working the room, thanking each person for taking precious time to come and share in our celebration. It is tough sometimes to have a conversation with every guest when it is a two-hour party and 300 people. The idea of going through your client database and deciding to plan smaller events with a select group of people you feel know one another or have many things in common can mean more quality time, for sure.

NATIONAL TV DEBUTS PACK THE HOUSE

Game night—I love this idea because it is so stinking simple! Pop some popcorn and have some drinks on hand. You can encourage everyone to bring their favorite game and a snack. Nothing beats the purity of a good ole' fashioned game night.

We have a swimming pool! We love having Potluck Pool parties! Bring your favorite snack, drink, and towel and come on! This is a fun way to relax and connect with clients, plus it's very kid friendly! I have always struggled with being as open to entertaining a lot during the summer because we work so many hours in the spring and summer months, when for a lot of people, it is their chill and vacation modes. Having everyone bring a snack, their favorite drinks, and most of all, their own beach towel, leaves me feeling less overwhelmed! I am not left trying to do several loads of laundry. If you don't have your own pool in your backyard, there are other options. Does your neighborhood have a pool or clubhouse you can rent out? Or do you have a community pool you could have everyone just meet at? It does not have to be a large number of people.

Dinner Cruise- We have a cool experience to offer clients here in Oklahoma City. It is something different too, and several folks have never had the opportunity to enjoy this kind of night out enjoying some phenomenal Oklahoma sunsets. They offer some fantastic specialty cruises such as Cocktail Cruises, Mother's Day, Father's Day, and Haunt the River. The best part is they are very reasonable in our city. Twenty to thirty dollars a person is not bad for snacks and cocktails.

Tea Party—You can get out your finest china that you hardly ever dust off and serve tea and simple pastries. (This is where I would be calling on my favorite baker, also a client, to provide the bunchkins for our party). I would help market her business to anyone that showed interest. You can have a Mommy and Me Tea or just have a grown-up ladies tea. Saturday afternoon is a great time. Always photograph and document the day. You can send out or share an album and ask people to share and add the hashtag of your choosing for amplified exposure.

Paint Party—This is an idea I want to do this fall. I will host a ladies' wine and palette party. There are complete party kits on Amazon, or you could always buy the items separately. I am a one and done type of gal, so I want the most time-efficient path possible. You can have all your guests bring their favorite bottle of wine and you provide the supplies and some light snacks. Easy-peasy, and it is something different we don't get to do often. I am the queen of frugality. I found there are some free painting tutorials you can play at the party or hire an instructor. You may have someone in your sphere that is talented who could volunteer to teach the group to paint something simple.

Movie Night—You can rent out a local theater and buy a bulk group rate of popcorn and a drink combo, then hand out vouchers. This can be a little expensive, but remember if you are a realtor, we negotiate for a living. It can't hurt to ask for a better deal than they are offering. It is cool if you can get a movie premiere of a really anticipated movie.

Scavenger Hunt—Did you know that there are literally tons of apps you can download for scavenger hunts? You can also google a bunch of printable hunts and even choose from different categories.

Berry picking—Berry picking farms are the rage in Oklahoma. It is such a fun, interactive activity to do with kiddos, or a cute little date with your honey. We photograph everyone at the farm during the picking activity so we can help everyone document the special day. Make sure to ask people to always tag and share your hashtag when they post on social media. Picking berries is fun but going home and continuing the experience when making homemade jam is even better. You can build memories by picking and canning! What a fun way to bond with kids and adults.

BO BERRY PICKING

Ladies Brunch—We have an entertaining home. We have two dining rooms and luckily, my husband is a master chef. This is a simple event. We have an easy casserole or quiche and some sparkling mimosas. Our goal is to spoil the ladies to a stress-free morning. We have two chair massage stations set up and the ladies can alternate having a light chair massage.

Vision Board Party—A vision board is a visualization tool which refers to a board of any sort used to build a collage of words and pictures that represent your goals and dreams. This is such a fun, cheap idea to gather together on a more intimate level. I invite about five ladies over. We have a few snacks and wine, everyone brings magazines, glue, scissors, and white poster board (You can use a cork board too if you like). Have everyone bring a bottle of wine and their favorite snack to make it stress-free to host if you are time broke. Encourage the participants to think about different things they want to learn, hobbies you currently love, relationships, career goals, and charity organizations that you are passionate about. How do you want to be remembered? Use personal photos or magazine clippings. It is really incredible to be a part of discussing our goals, hopes, and dreams and putting them on a visual platform to focus on daily! Talk about a bonding experience. You will really get to know others well and on a deeper level when you do an intimate activity like this.

I love this quote by Jack Canfield. "Your brain will work tirelessly to achieve the statements you give your subconscious mind. And when those statements are the affirmations and images of your goals, you are destined to achieve them!" – Jack Canfield

This is not a place you have your sales hat on! Your only focus is working the room to get quality time with each of your clients who took the time to come.

Planning these parties takes a very organized, structured person. If that is not you, assign that role to someone else so it can be as successful as possible. From start to finish, each and every detail truly matters! People are so busy!

We have a systematic approach: send an evite invitation, then a paper invitation we have mailed out, an event created on Facebook, Slydial announcing to save the date, followed up with personal calls, and the day before the party send a mass reminder text (that comes from our phone number). After the party, we sent a handwritten thank you card for their cherished attendance.

This are seven touches inside this one event. And the touches are only because we want to show our people how much we appreciate them.

We want nothing from them. Coming from a pure place of contribution will bless you in the end. You can ask sponsors to contribute to the party or donate gift cards, etc. (Check for your local regulations/RESPA laws). We oftentimes don't involve sponsors because we want the vibe that we are asking for nothing in return. If a vendor is there and wants to say a few words or I do a pitch when I am drawing for a prize they sponsored, it starts feeling salesy.

I would rather have an experience than a tangible gift. An experience is a way to make lasting memories. You can always ask for your preferred vendors to help sponsor your events. Remember, you will need to brand all your invites, etc., reflecting their sponsorship and giving them an opportunity to give a quick elevator speech on their service and offerings. You always want to express your utmost appreciation and gratitude for their contribution. You want to share your enthusiasm and commitment in helping them build their businesses and fulfill their dreams.

When we do our two larger client appreciation events, we have a videographer come and set up in a private room. He is available for our clients to step in and do a quick video testimonial. This is not something we pressure people to do. Your clients who love the spotlight and enjoy sharing their stories will voluntarily and gleefully give a video testimony.

Start small if you need to but start somewhere. You really can do these events on a shoestring budget and build from there. You can always rent a neighborhood clubhouse or a builder's model home, with permission and liability waivers, of course. There is no better way to ingrain in your customers how special and adored they are than to create a night ALL about them!

Chapter 23
Customer Spotlight!

I have found another simple, yet poignant way to stay engaged with your client well after the transaction. (I also mention spotlighting and advocating for your preferred vendors as well.) They are a member of your tribe, after all. If you are staying in touch, continuing to show value and credibility, you will surely be top of mind for referrals and personal real estate dealings.

So, what does a customer spotlight look like?

As I have mentioned before, each one of our clients has their own unique story! It may be the reason why they bought or sold, that they bought their dream home, or focus on them as amazing humans. Many of our clients have their own businesses and we love supporting them and helping them grow! Change it up depending on the client and the story behind their life! Also, when you make the call to let them know they are being featured as a customer spotlight, ask them what they would like to share. For example, we have a buyer that is a house flipper. He may very well show us his remodel or take us on site to show us some of his work. It may be a couple who just got married and we can recap their love story! Another example is a buyer who purchased her house about five years ago. She recently messaged me to tell me she is now in remission, and I thought how cool it would be to show up at her doorstep and bring her balloons and flowers to celebrate such a miracle and milestone! She does not have a business, but she has a story I can and want to celebrate! The stories are endless. Each person we do business with results in a relationship, so it does not feel like work keeping in touch. It is part of nurturing our friendship, which is what the relationship organically becomes.

My most favorite spotlights are when I am in an establishment and I spontaneously start videoing and raving about the business.

Managers/owners love the free publicity and are tickled pink you want to share it with your tribe. Not everyone loves to be put on the spot and be on camera. Some will surprise you and eat it up. Just roll with it! These business owners do not soon forget that you not only value their service, but you are shouting it from the rooftop to help them grow!

Spending more time focusing on your customers and the stories they represent is much more rewarding than shamelessly bragging about yourself. When your intentions and your heart are customer-centric and focused on giving to others, you will be blessed ten-fold. Be consistent when you start a system of recognizing your customers.

What are your favorite businesses? Compile a list!

Who can you spotlight?

Who can you help boost their business, extend a genuine act of kindness, or celebrate in some way?

Chapter 24
Supersize that service and add Ala carte!

Ever heard the saying it is all in the details? It is so true. Little things can mean the most and make the biggest impressions. Here are a few tips for going the extra mile.

Bring fresh cut flowers to the photography appointment or the day you list the home. There is something so homey and aromatic about the smell of fresh flowers right when you step into a home. Not to mention aesthetically they look colorful and inviting.

If the curb appeal is lacking, pick up a colorful pot and fill with some vibrant flowers to spruce up the appeal from the street. We all know buyers typically see the home online and then drive by to get a feel for the area and neighborhood. Make those buyers fall in love at the curb!

Encourage your sellers to have soft, soothing music playing during showings. Music relaxes and calms people. When buyers are house hunting, oftentimes it is overwhelming and stressful. Do whatever you can in the home to provide a tranquil, peaceful vibe to the environment.

When we take buyers out house hunting, it is ALL about them! When they step into our vehicle, they are being served. We invite them to pick the music we play in the car and have ice cold waters in the seat holders. We bring a small ice chest with drinks and light snacks. House hunting often feels like a sport—a sport I wear stilettos to do! We go fast and we want to offer a level of service and hospitality like no other. We love kids of all ages, which comes in handy when a family needs to bring kids along on the house hunt. We always offer to help with the kids. This is the biggest investment most people make in their lifetime; we want the decision makers to be able to focus as much as possible. Being hospitable and accommodating is not easily forgotten. We are more than merely the person who can get the key out of a lockbox.

We are implicitly trusted to guide and advocate for our clients as they are making some of the most monumental decisions of their lives.

One example to level up and exceed expectations of the norm is the time an elderly seller needed to touch-up chipped paint around her garage. She did not have the original paint and was very stressed. To most, this is not a daunting task, but to her it was. Send a handyman over to do it or take it upon yourself to go get a paint match, a quart of paint, and just do it. You'd have a client for life by taking care of something so simple yet so overwhelming to your seller.

Many of us are just so tapped out and time broke! You might be asking yourself how you can be everything to all your clients when your own home is neglected due to lack of time. If that is the case, build a good relationship with an outstanding handyman who extends service the way you do and call on them to do a few small things when they present themselves. When our eyes are wide open on a quest to anticipate and recognize the needs of others, there are ample opportunities.

What extras can you offer on your menu of services?

What can you do to truly transcend expectations?

To drill down even more and take it a step further, listen up! I recently finished reading the book *Customers for Life*, by Carl Sewell and Paul B. Brown. They mention in the book that there are certain services they offer for free. Carl is in the luxury car business with his dealership selling Cadillacs. He mentioned if a customer calls the shop and has a flat tire, one of his servicemen goes and changes it for FREE. He goes on to state their motto, "Is this something a friend would charge for?" This is such a powerful question, and it truly resonates with me. The dealership prides themselves on offering what I like to call extra ala carte services that create customers for life. I can't personally change a tire. If you came to my rescue, put my spare on, and took my tire for repair for NO CHARGE, I would become a raving fan for life. That is a story I repeat to all my friends and family and blast all over social media. Whenever I get asked about a car dealership I recommend, I would shout it from the mountaintop.

We had a client who was late to their final walk-through for the closing of their first home because they'd gotten a flat tire. They were stressed beyond belief. We offered to come help change the flat tire and asked their special request order from Chick-fil-A. They were absolutely thrilled! This was such an easy thing we could do to take a load off and get all their bellies full so they could focus on their move-in.

I learned so much in this book. Good is simply not good enough. We should always encourage honest feedback and make the customer comfortable giving it. Thank them for the negative feedback. It gives you an opportunity to apologize, then redesign the system to eliminate the flaw.

What extras can you offer as you go? What I mean by "as you go" is when needs reveal themselves to you or you anticipate needs your clients don't even verbalize.

Many of our buyers have full-time jobs, full plates, and empty energy tanks. Going house hunting with kids can be crazy. The chaos of chasing your children around repeating, "Don't touch that, it is not yours," is not fun. Or having the resounding quote, "You break it, you buy it," puts on an extra amount of pressure as well. The buyers oftentimes simply can't focus on the things they need to look at and investigate with a child in tow. Offer babysitting for your clients and everyone will thank you! You may have some clients decline, but it is a great extra to offer a fantastic babysitter and you will be the hero! Make sure your sitter comes highly recommended with first aid training and references to give full peace of mind to your clients.

BUILT-IN BABYSITTING---THE BEST CARPET PAD
QUALITY TESTERS RIGHT HERE

https://www.propertyme.com.au/blog/property-
management/proven-ways-to-make-your-listing-stand-out

https://placester.com/real-estate-marketing-academy/creative-real-
estate-marketing-ideas-listings/

Getting serious about Funny!

CLOWNING AROUND

It is no wives' tale; laughter is the best medicine. It is like oxygen. It is a natural stress reliever, fights depression, and is even a calorie burning workout! Who wants to do a hundred sit ups a day? I would much rather hang out with people who make me laugh. I am not just talking about a chuckle, but a big belly-laugh from my gut. That could help you burn as much as thirty-five calories an hour. It is better than a kick in the pants and much easier than a sit up. Incorporating humor in your business and organization is vital and creates a cohesive feel to your group resulting in everyone having a sense of belonging. We believe in this so much that we have incorporated a "giggle break." We either work on humor-infused marketing content or watch a funny video. Laughter energizes you and recharges your soul. There is a stat that proves people with a sense of humor tend to be more productive. Maybe that is why I get so much done!

You know when you see ads for any pharmaceutical medicines there are a bunch of horrific side effects. Humor is like a medicine with no bad side effects. It is a pure way to connect with others and create an endless list of benefits for the culture of your company and organization.

There is a difference between being funny and being snarky. Ask yourself questions to ensure you are not crossing boundaries with your humor.

*Is this targeting anyone else? Don't make others the butt of your jokes. I break this rule daily with Troy. He is my husband so I have a free pass, but others are off limits. Making fun of others and publicly embarrassing anyone followed by the famous words, "just kidding," does not qualify you as a well-received comedian in your office.

*Could your grandmother look at this post and not be offended?

Don't be afraid to be vulnerable and self-deprecating. We do not take ourselves too seriously. Having your colleagues be comfortable expressing humor is a game changer. Jesse Cole, author of *Find Your Yellow Tux*, has an "Ideapalooza" meeting. All his staff can submit ideas, anonymously or not. They sit around the table with a fire in their bellies and mastermind over each and every idea. There are no bad ideas. They have three bucket categories:

#1 YES- absolutely implementing

#2 Needs a little work (maybe more resources)

#3 Maybe later- tabled but not ruled out

There is definitely power in numbers when thinking about collaboration. Something magical occurs when people feel encouraged to throw vulnerability out the window and share an idea. I might have a fragment of an idea, and once ten other people start feeding on it, we can pull a full-blown marketing success story from it. We are all in this together. The beauty is we are all different. We have different hobbies, interests, family backgrounds, diverse exposures to pop culture and all things trending. Bringing people to the melting pot where ideas are generated, and then watching them flourish and grow into something spellbinding is nothing short of amazing. No one person needs to take credit, allow it to be a culture of team efforts where you all equally feel you are an integral part of bringing it together. This approach will foster a genuine team effort in all projects.

If someone comes to the table and submits an idea that is unanimously accepted, allow that person to be an Idea Champion. They can be the CEO of that idea and help form a team to make it come to fruition.

One of the ways to bring humor into the workplace is to have friendly competitions. Laughter and humor ignite creativity and frees your mind to create and innovate.

Implement a Fun Committee! YES, a fun committee. You have a committee for growth, finances, marketing, social/holiday events, why not fun? There is a running joke with Troy and I that he is the CEO and CFO, and I am the Director of Fun! It is not a dirty word at work! There is a time and a place. I am not saying go to work and do nothing but go from cubicle to cubicle telling knock-knock jokes or shooting a water gun on the guy in the corner office with his door open. Creating white space for fun and humor does not negate our responsibilities to be productive. It does the opposite!

Contests for the person with the most embarrassing moment!

Have a Funniest Halloween Costume contest (theme contests are really fun and work well for content creation for social media holiday posts, etc.)

Have a dress like your boss day! (This one just came to mind; don't tell your boss the staff is planning this one. Keep it on the down low for a surprise factor!)

Bring your pet to work day! Pet must dress like the employee! Provide ties or a feminine accessory for the animals! You might be cautious about this one as some people have crazy pets. I don't necessarily want a snake or a pig at the office for nine hours! With the popularity of chickens, who knows what your staff would bring. On the other hand, the more unique the pet, the better the marketing content surrounding these special days. Ultimately you know what will be feasible in your workspace. Have fun with it!

KIKI THE CLOSER MAKES AN APPEARANCE AT SOME CLOSINGS AND SHOWINGS

Bring your kid to work day! Yes, make this a thing! Have the kids dress like their mom or dad and create a whole content marketing day out of it! Do a photo shoot of the kids with their parents, create a hashtag, and ask your employees to share on all their social media platforms as well as the company's business pages, etc. Get video coverage of the kids at the conference table with mom or dad and ask the kids questions about what their parents do at work. What do the kids want to do when they grow up, and so on. The content I share around kids is so organic, raw, and straight up hilarious.

OWEN ASHFORD, EXECUTIVE IN TRAINING

You could also have an office pet! I love dressing up our animals! It must come from my love for fashion in general. You could have some branded ensembles for the pet to wear around the office. (Check up to ensure none of your employees are allergic to any furry animals or it could pose a problem.) Pets can reduce blood pressure and create a feeling of home in the workplace. We often spend more time at our jobs than we do our home!

INCORPORATING PETS IN YOUR MARKETING IS FUN AND ENDEARING IF YOUR PET IS UP FOR THE CHALLENGE

Give a trophy out for your employee who has dealt with the most stress that week and really made it work.

Have a Dance Break! Learn an easy team dance that does not require coordination but gives you some content to share about your company having fun. TikTok makes this so fun! It is an up-and-coming app and there is room to dominate! Fostering a fun climate in your workplace attracts people. Working hard and playing hard is my motto. When you interview people, make a sense of humor at the top of your checklist for new hires. Make sure they are not just aligned in work ethic and skill sets but are open to letting loose and matching the culture you want to craft in your organization.

Another cool idea would be making a bet! Make a friendly competition over who can attain or retain the most accounts for the month. Commonly people do March Madness boards, Weight loss challenges, Super Bowl bets. We do an Oscar Winner bet annually and it is so fun for the movie/Hollywood buffs. I am not talking about the kind of bets that get your clothes thrown out on the lawn because your partner is peeved about a bet. A few bucks is fine so everyone can get involved and feel a sense of being included. The loser has to dress in a silly costume of the winner's choice. The bet can involve any wager that will breed laughter and infuse fun throughout your entire office.

There is nothing worse than the dread of setting that alarm and getting up for work on Monday morning. Give your employees something fun to look forward to regularly. There is a company called Watercooler Trivia. Their mission is to build team culture, one trivia contest at a time. The whole idea is to spark conversations, celebrate the winners, and make the work week more fun! Participants submit their responses at any point during the day and then the results are delivered right to the inbox the next morning. They even rate who had the funniest answer! Whoever wins gets a cool, quirky prize! The first four weeks are free to try so you can get feedback from your staff.

My mother passed and had a stuffed toy lamb that my sister and I exchange every six months. We call it Sisterhood of the Traveling Lamb (instead of Pants). Why not create a mascot that gets passed to an employee of the month? They could get a special, designated parking place and have to carry the stuffed animal to every meeting that month! Something silly becomes an item of prestige and honor.

CLAIRE HANDING OVER THE SISTERHOOD OF THE TRAVELING LAMB

Build team culture conversations.

At our real estate brokerage, they present the Red Shoe Award, and you get possession of a red Converse for the month! It is an award for being kind and helping others at a high level.

RED SHOE CULTURE AWARD

For birthdays, do something out of the norm. Give your staff members the option to choose a day off from the remainder of the year. Present cupcakes or their favorite sweet treat. Have a red carpet rolled out leading into their office and a crown or tiara they wear for the day! Making people feel valued and appreciated through recognition is far better than a store-bought gift or a gift card, which screams there was little thought or creativity put into it.

Just as important as birthdays are, anniversaries simply cannot be forgotten! Have a unique way to celebrate. Have a chair masseuse come in for a fun idea. My favorite is a tailored singing telegram! The key is knowing your people. Who is their favorite superhero or actor/actress? It can get costly having to purchase a different costume for each staff member, but the reactions are priceless! How cool is it when your employees post all your birthday surprises and show their royal treatment? It will definitely create some buzz about your company being one that treats their employees like royalty.

Stress is inevitable! Why not spoil your people at any given opportunity when they are performing at optimal levels.

Decorate your break room with humorous posters! Have a whiteboard for the joke of the day or word of the day, all comedic in nature. Set the tone for joy and laughter in your office! You have to create the culture! Have a table where there are some stress relieving items or games. You could provide Jenga, stress balls, small ping pong tables, foosball, sand trays, basketball hoops, or jigsaws. The rage now is indoor swings! People love these! Nothing like jumping on a swing for a little childhood nostalgia, sipping your soft drink during your break to clear your mind before getting back to the grind.

Create a culture where sharing successes and picking one another up after a failure is the norm. The power of collaborating within a team environment can be pivotal in having a sense of unity versus catty, cutthroat competition that soils your economy or fills the workplace with toxicity. Celebrate when others win! When a baby is born at our local hospital, a lullaby is always played. When someone books an appointment, gets a new contract executed, etc., have a bell you let them ring! Use it for content on social media! Don't just ring the bell, include in your video a story about the client or why this family is special. Bring it back to showing the story of your clients.

Architect a plan where a team member's accomplishments are loudly recognized and your extreme appreciation for their efforts are always expressed.

A creativity award is awesome! I would rather have a most creative or most innovative award than anything else! Do something fun to celebrate this honor! Have a caricaturist come in and do a drawing and then display it proudly in your break room or conference room.

For staff meetings, start out by going around the room and having everyone state one positive thing that has happened that week with a client. How were you able to woo a client in a profound way to gain a client for life? When you start your staff meetings off this way every time, it builds a culture in which your people will seek ways to woo, win, and wow clients. It will always be top of mind because it is the first item on your agenda, showing it is a priority in your culture.

The most meaningful exercise I have ever been a part of in a class was a simple one. We all taped a piece of paper to our back, and everyone wrote something kind and positive about you on the paper. I still have the paper where we did this about my second year in real estate. A veteran agent that is a powerhouse, to say the least, wrote something on my paper I will never forget. He wrote, "You are the real deal, a true mega agent!" Someone could have written I was the fairest one of all a hundred times and would not have touched my heartstrings the way this did. In my life, I struggled and treaded water tirelessly trying to find myself and feel valued in a career path. For this agent who I highly respected to tell me I impressed him was a paradigm shift. The power of words is so important. We need to show our people that we deeply appreciate them, and not just on special occasions.

Have you ever heard about music breaks? At regular intervals, blast music for a few minutes on your intercom or shoot a message on IM or email. Play something that really gets everyone's energy up! I strongly suggest these breaks for afternoon when you sometimes hit a wall and would rather take a corporate nap than get jazzed up. Let it be a reminder for your employees to get up, stretch, walk, take a few-minute break to recharge and interrupt that food coma we often land in after a carb-filled lunch.

Before a staff meeting, watch a funny video, play a game that gets everyone's guards down and energy up.

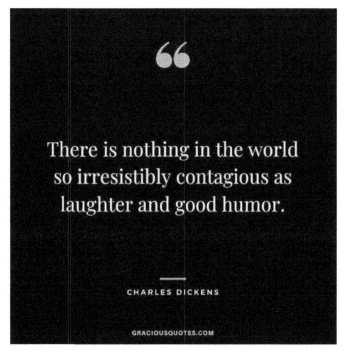

CHARLES DICKENS

GRACIOUSQUOTES.COM

Create a #hashtag for your organization. Encourage your team to always use the hashtag and tag others so you receive as much buzz and momentum as possible.

Implement a Vent box and Bright Idea Box in your break room or a way you can anonymously submit. Foster a collaborative environment and the sky's the limit. We all have different perspectives, ideas, opinions and can all learn from the diversity within the group. There is so much beauty in our differences and what each individual brings to the table. Allow people to have credit for their suggestions and be rewarded and recognized for accomplishments and goals met. Developing a culture where there are no junk ideas will help people feel freer to share one. Odds are if there is a deep collaboration, you can make even the worst idea into something fantastic just by openly masterminding. There is a saying, "Always be closing." "Always be thanking" is mine. If there is an opportunity to acknowledge someone, don't just think it, say it! It is such a cool thing when you are recognized in front of the other staff, not just privately.

I am currently practicing what I preach, taking humor to an all-time high! I got nominated by my sister to be on a season of the *Worst Cooks in America*. The Food Network has a show especially for losers like me that are epic fails in the kitchen. I can do so many things really well. I am a jack of all trades, if you will. Cooking is not one of them. The best skill I have in the kitchen is kissing the cook! I was game to literally learn how to cook on national television. I had never watched the show, but once I did, I was all in! It is a comedy, but contestants are serious as a heart attack over the competition to win $25,000. I had to cook on camera for my audition. We were about to move in less than a week, so I had literally NO cookware not packed up. In fact, the kitchen stuff was the first stuff I had packed because it is not used often due to my poor cooking skills. I ended up not even having a potholder, so I improvised and used a paper towel to lift a pot. This was not the brightest thing to do because it went up in flames. Troy was filming it and hysterically telling me to get water on it. You could clearly see it was not staged but was a completely unscripted disaster in the kitchen. I have never felt more vulnerable than being in this cast of the show. There were fourteen of us hand-selected from thousands of entries of the worst of the worst. It is safe to say I was the Real Housewife of the kitchen and just needed to stick to selling kitchens, not cooking in them. It is still not my forte'. You can now say I am not the worst cook in all of America, but like the fourth worst. Being able to make fun of yourself in a self-deprecating way is something I have always incorporated in our marketing. Peeling back layers and not portraying yourself as perfect is vital to connecting with others.

My airtime on this show gave me all new material to display on my social media! Anytime I have had television, press releases, human interest stories etc., I always bring it back to the fact that I am a realtor. I reference being a realtor many times throughout the show, plus my profession is on my ticker under my name during my outtake segments. I was featured in newspapers and even real estate sections of papers, even though it is not real estate related. A local realtor is being featured on one of the top-rated shows on a major network. These are stories reporters crave. They are out of the norm and attract attention, no matter what industry.

I was in a cast of some of the most diverse, big personality people on the planet. I have never had an experience like this where you were able to grow so close to the castmates. Not having electronic devices the majority of the time breeds getting to know each other on a very deep level. It was interesting because I usually have one of the biggest personalities in the room, but I had to earn my right in this one. I can now see how wrapped up you can become with each other and connected for life after having an experience like this. In any television opportunity I have had, I always sprinkle in the fact that I am a realtor in the narrative. For this particular show, they will flash my name and profession on the screen. This is better than a billboard. *Worst Cooks in America* is one of the highest-ranking shows on the Food Network. Maximizing exposure from these appearances has been instrumental in gaining name recognition and branding. When people think of us, they think top realtors and frequently featured on high rated shows and networks.

DENISE FAWN SCHRODER

NEWSPAPER PUBLICITY PHOTO FOR
WORST COOKS IN AMERICA

SEASON 20 CAST FOOD NETWORK,
WORST COOKS IN AMERICA

CHEF ANNE BURRELL INSTILLING IN ME THAT I AM A
BEAST IN THE KITCHEN

NEWSPAPER CLIPPING PROMOTING
WORST COOKS IN AMERICA

I got a call this week from the *Ellen Game of Games*. The casting producer said they scoured our social media and think we are hilarious. Game OVER. The fact that a comedic show did a forensic audit on who we are and love our energy and ability to connect is surreal to me. Capturing the attention of major network shows never gets old! STOP THE SCROLL! Using humor blended with vulnerability is such a powerful recipe!

As I mention also in the publication chapter, one of the first headlines in the news was "Oklahoma City real estate sales team uses humor to sell homes." We are still using humor and wit in all our marketing and media/ television/radio opportunities. This headline meant a lot to me because the article featured a statement I said that rings so true. "Our marketing may seem out of the box, quirky, fun-spirited, but make no mistake, this team gets results and performs at a high level and will continue to dominate the market." We have perfected a balanced recipe of marketing and displaying results and credibility along with showing people who we really are. We are not a cookie cutter, copy and paste brand. We are just us. When you get to the point where you have the confidence and freedom to be YOU, the money naturally follows. We have had many realtors imitate us and copy ideas. That is the biggest form of flattery.

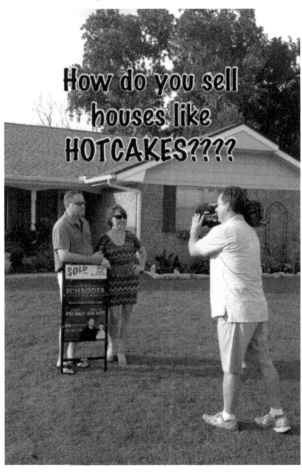

LIVE, ON THE SCENE

FUN MARKETING AND CLOSING PHOTOS FOR OUR CLIENTS KEEPSAKES AND SOCIAL MEDIA

Employee turnover is costly and stressful on you and your employees. Create an atmosphere where people respect you and want to give a hundred and fifty percent and always be on their A game, but also carve out the time for your people to have fun! If you would like to explore the culture of your company, send out an anonymous SurveyMonkey questionnaire and encourage your staff to be transparent and completely honest. If you have focused on the climate in the workplace where you have instilled collaboration, celebration, appreciation, and transparency, your treasured staff will feel more open to share without feeling they will be penalized. You can't just send the surveys out; you need to commit to actively listening and doing your best to implement improvements so your staff knows they are heard.

When passionate people become quiet, there is a problem. People don't leave their jobs; they leave poor managers. It is oftentimes less about the money and more about how people are treated when they choose to sever ties and quit.

How can you implement some fun and humor in your workplace? If you are not the boss, go to your supervisor and brainstorm how to inject some powerful ways to have more fun at work while being highly productive and building stronger relationships. It is a win-win!

https://www.laughterremedy.com/article_pdfs/Ideas%20for%20Ma king%20work%20Fun.pdf

https://www.humorthatworks.com/benefits/30-benefits-of-humor-at-work/

https://www.linkedin.com/pulse/40-fun-office-game-ideas-engage-employees-susanna-varghese/

https://www.outbackteambuilding.com/blog/10-ideas-to-make-your-office-break-room-better-for-employees/

Get Reel!

Anytime we do video content, the process of the entire production footage is far better than the actual photo or video on script. I invested in a tripod I take literally everywhere I go. We were recently reenacting a meme. We did not have anyone to get the money shot, so we knew we would have to video it and still screenshot the best shot. It ended up being funnier than the actual meme itself. We have had more spontaneous moments while doing a video of ourselves or our clients. At times, our clients think we are taking a picture of them trying to get a pose or a dance move right and we are actually doing a video. It is so hilarious to see people organically doing something when they do not know they are on camera. It is seriously like the show *Candid Camera*.

When I am doing a video and have to start over several times or stutter or mess up, sometimes even fall, we keep rolling. Consumers don't want a perfect, commercial-vibe video. Consumers want to connect. Draw them in with an authentic, uninhibited approach. Let go and let your guard down. Much more effective than stopping a scroll and a quick like.

Humor is so important to us and bringing smiles and giggles to others is the icing on the cake. Bloopers are better than the finished product in almost all cases to me!

How can you push yourself out of your comfort zone and embrace it?

If you are uncomfortable, you are growing!

Meme Mimic

I am absolutely obsessed with memes! I have started this new thing called Meme Mimic! It is so much fun and we get an overwhelmingly fun response on social media. Why? People like to laugh, and they love self-deprecating humor! The video we create of the whole process is better than the actual finished product, if you can believe it!

You should try a humorous post for yourself and get a feel for the feedback you get! Our audience loves them! I can't wait to make some more creations! Try creating a meme about something relevant and well-known in pop culture to really connect and collect giggles.

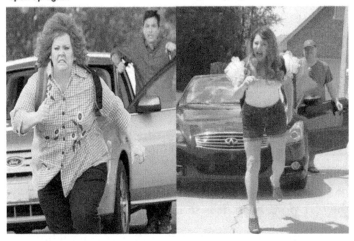

AFTER COVID, THIS WAS A GENUINE FEELING, LOL!

A VARIETY OF FUNNY MEME MIMICS

We have started experimenting with TikTok. Or let's just say, I come up with nutty ideas that I beg Troy to do with me. It takes great effort to get this done, but when we do, it is so worth it!

Yet another opportunity to step out of your comfort zone and playfully engage with your audience! Realtors and small businesses are jumping in feet first to create their own lane and find a niche in this space that breeds creativity.

What the Flock?

Have you ever thought about what our actions would look like if we first thought to ourselves, "How can I make someone feel appreciated?" Most of my ideas come from a genuine place of wanting to create a lasting impression on our clients. Creating these WOO moments are so fun, and I can't ever get enough! You already know handwritten cards are a daily priority. I came up with the idea to draw randomly from our clients and flock their yard. I have seen flocking for years on very special occasions, filling someone's front yard with a flock of birds like flamingos. Our concept is different from the traditional flocking fundraiser order of things. We also don't use flamingos. Why? Because we don't want to be the norm, we want to do things that are completely different. You will never hear someone describe us or our business as normal or traditional. That is why we choose Smiley Faces! We call the campaign Schroder Smiles! It is to the point! We flock with a message of appreciation from our group with the hope that we can create a smile and bring some joy into the lives of others.

I love getting the phone calls as people are genuinely surprised when they look out the window or go to check their mail. The whole purpose we do this as part of our business model is to take those opportunities to create these WOO moments with people! Schroder Smiles campaign is one of my favorites. It is just a fun, out-of-the-box way to let your people know you are thinking about them and appreciate them, with no strings attached!

I challenge you to think of things you can do to express nothing but appreciation and gratitude for others. It certainly does not need to be as radical as flocking a yard. A simple text, call, or Facebook message instilling hope and care sometimes can impact another more than you realize.

What can you do to create a WOO moment that gives your customer something to talk about?

YARD FLOCKING

Chapter 25
Hot off the Press

My love for writing has come in handy. I swear my middle name is "publicity." A beloved friend called me a shameless self-promoter. There is an art to not coming off as vain, for sure. I have been writing human-interest stories and press releases since my early twenties. I really focused on this when I started a pet sitting business in the city I lived in. I can remember when I was trying to create my name for my LLC, I had so many cute, foo-foo names and a great logo with an animated lady with high heels walking several dogs. My grandpa said to me, "Denise, you need to keep it simple. Make it something that is a no-brainer, and the consumer won't forget." That is when "My Pet Sitter, LLC" was born. It was simple, but it anchored exactly what service I provided. At the time I worked at a women's hospital as a surgery tech. The physicians worked hard, but vacations were a priority. I was the saving grace so the pets did not have to be boarded. Oftentimes, the pets come home with fleas or dietary issues after spending time with a lot of strange animals and different types of food outside their normal diet. I wrote a human-interest story and pitched it to several local publications. I got a call from a reporter right away who wanted to feature my new company as a spotlight business, filling the gap in our town for a much-needed service. This was incredible, free exposure for me to attain new clients.

MY PETSITTER PUBLICATION ARTICLE

Newspapers are always looking for great, local content. Sometimes when I send something into the publications or directly to a journalist, they will take my copy and just paste it. Other times, it induces an actual phone, zoom/skype, or sit-down interview. Not only am I getting free exposure, but I am able to communicate and connect with the writers, journalists, etc., and they often become customers or raving fans. Better yet, they look to me to become a resource for future articles and content.

I was my own relentless publicist for getting my own kids in the paper countless times when going to community events. When I worked for a local public school system, I used to get all our school activities submitted and invite reporters and photographers to come cover it personally! It is safe to say, publicity is definitely in my DNA. I have always had a love for storytelling and photography. My philosophy is no matter what you do in your career, you don't just show up. You show up and perform. I was listening to a podcast recently. James Gilmore said every business is a theater and a show. Be aware the experience is being witnessed. Every second someone is watching! Present yourself in a way that journalists, editors, producers, and directors know without a shadow of a doubt their audience will eat your content up and beg for more.

When I worked for a local school system, I added publicist on the daunting list of my job description. I worked very hard to submit quality happenings at the school to be shared with our community. Below are some of the incredible staff dressed up for Halloween and an end of the year production we put on.

Prom Chaperones
Yukon High School staff members serve as chaperones for Saturday night's annual YHS Prom at the Ballroom of the University of Central Oklahoma in Edmond: From left, YHS 9-10 Assistant Principal Joe Meziere, YHS 11-12 Assistant Principal Charlotte Blevins, and YHS 11-12 Principal Dylon Coleman along with Denise McPherson, and Paula and Jason Glass.

At the Prom
Yukon High School staff members enjoy the annual YHS Prom at the University of Central Oklahoma in Edmond: From left, Denise McPherson, YHS 11-12 Assistant Principal Mark Melton, Marti Brown, and YHS 11-12 Assistant Principal Charlotte Blevins.

YUKON HIGH SCHOOL PROM PUBLICATION
I SUBMITTED

Troy and I also have had a photography business. We both loved photography. My grandfather took pictures of every single moment of our lives, literally. He is the reason why you can never catch me in a candid shot. I am hyper aware of the camera due to my grandfather always having it ready to capture moments. My obsession with documenting and storytelling is a deep-seated one. Whenever I look through the lens, I employ a marketing strategist mindset. This drives everyone around me crazy. If it were up to me, we would have video cameras everywhere in our home and car. Heck, we would even have body cams! Working together with our office based out of our home leads to some raw, funny, and transparent moments in the day. I have even purchased secret eyeglass cameras and a rearview mirror cam for the car.

Use your gifts to give and the fruits will come. We donated our time and talents to a good cause, and in turn were really blessed beyond measure.

We were asked to donate our time to take photos for a fundraising event in 2012. Russell Westbrook of the OKC Thunder was the spokesman. If you do not follow NBA Basketball, he is one of the greatest players of all time. He was the absolute heartbeat of our Oklahoma City Thunder team. I was squealing at the thought of meeting Russ in the flesh! The organization was the Needs Foundation. Needs Foundation is a 501(c)3 charitable non-profit that collects the un-served or unsold food surplus from grocers, bakeries, and restaurants, and distributes the food to needy Oklahomans through community programs, churches, community centers, group homes, schools, and food pantries.

The event was held at the former Governor's Mansion, a red-carpet affair with a massive turnout. There was a meet and greet and a big auction. Russell Westbrook is the heartbeat of our NBA OKC Thunder basketball team. It was amazing to see the people bringing in basketballs, shirts, jerseys, etc., for Russ to autograph. I can remember calling my sister-in-law to go quickly buy a basketball so we could have it signed for our son, who was one of Westbrook's biggest fans! I was told by the party organizer that I needed to meet Russ in the study and take his photos. I am sure I had a deer-in-headlights kind of blank stare on my face. Who? Me? I later got a text from his publicist stating she needed the edited photos back asap. They needed to be submitted to ESPN and other outlets for the story about his work as a spokesman for such an incredible local cause. I can remember walking in the study to photograph him along with another photographer taking photos for a local publication.

Russell asked me why I looked nervous! He said, "Look at this guy," pointing to the other photographer who had Velcro tennis shoes, a funny combover, and seemed very awkward. "You got this." He was doing everything he could to get us to laugh and encouraging me that it was all good.

We had a great photo session, and I submitted all the photos from the event to the local papers. I was absolutely flabbergasted at the magnitude of photos they shared. We had just started in real estate and did not have near the confidence we have today. I submitted the press release/human interest story to my favorite real estate journalist. He was happy to do a huge story. The picture of Russell and me was massive, and others of Troy and myself on the red carpet and other event photos made a fantastic story to bring awareness to the organization, and we are listed in the article as local realtors. Three other local papers also ran the story!

Thunder star helps aid hunger relief in Oklahoma

Yukon's Troy and Denise Schroder chosen to photograph event featuring Russell Westbrook

RUSSELL WESTBROOK FUNDRAISER ARTICLE

Okarche native, wife appear on Steve Harvey show

By Tim Farley
News Editor

"You have to be unified in front of them. You might disagree behind closed doors but you have to remain arm-in-arm when they (children) see you."

Denise Schroder
Giving advice on blended families

Troy and Denise Schroder will appear on The Steve Harvey Show Friday, Feb. 10 as part of a panel on marriage. The couple, who own a real estate company in Yukon, also has appeared on House Hunters.

MORE PUBLICITY

I have a wall of most of our articles that have been featured and published. I love looking at them and reflecting how unbelievably blessed we have been. Newspapers and publications need content. Give them something to talk about. We have gotten so much free exposure in local papers and international publications, it seems surreal. You don't know unless you try. What do you have to lose? Advertising is not cheap. Most businesses in our industry don't do a lot of print advertising due to the cost, lack of R.O.I., and statistics showing it just doesn't bring in sales. So let the newspapers help you for free.

However, it goes back to the fact that stories stick, and everyone has one! Part of my creative mind knows that we must visually tell the story, not just with words and copy. Instead of telling everyone you and your team are so awesome, how about asking your clients to tell their story and how working with you made them feel. If you are approaching this the right way, you will get some incredible raw moments of people being vulnerable with you.

One of my favorite human interest stories was about a couple who was just under forty years old and purchasing their first home together. Justin and Alyssa were two of the most gracious people I have ever met. They had a childlike excitement about purchasing their home. They closed and got the keys a few days before Christmas. A couple of days before their highly anticipated home buying celebration, Justin's brother, only in his thirties, passed away from a complication during a routine procedure. I watched their hearts break as they were feeling overwhelmed, but at the same time so thankful to finally put down some roots and make their home. Even though we had just met, I felt such empathy for their loss and shared in their sheer joy and gratefulness to finally become homeowners.

GILLIAM STORY ARTICLE, DAILY OKLAHOMAN

Here is a display at one of our watch parties with our articles people could read to see our journey. This is not all of our articles, and you can see it has had astounding results. This has all been FREE!

DENISE AND TROY'S PUBLICITY NEWSPAPER CLIPPING DISPLAY

Seek to understand what your local media is reporting on and find a topic not being covered that would appeal to the audience. Start to submit content on a regular basis. You may not always have your articles approved for publication, but you are positioning yourself to be a trusted, thought leader in the industry. Your name will become more than a familiarity. When the local journalists, media, reporters, etc., need insight or a story, you will be top of mind. Media outlets are not just seeking content, they are looking for stories that stick!

NEWS 9 REAL EXPERT PIECE WITH NEWS 9, OKLAHOMA
DEANN MCGEHEE, REPORTER

OKLAHOMAN.COM WITH RICHARD MIZE CHATTING
ABOUT THE CURRENT REAL ESTATE MARKET

DAILY OKLAHOMA REAL ESTATE EXPERT ARTICLE

Chapter 26
Give them something to talk about!

Have you ever gotten a phone call that just catapults you into the goofiest happy dance and sheer state of euphoria you have ever seen? I got that call from Richard Mize, then real estate editor for The Oklahoman and Oklahoman.com. He is a hustler, to say the least. He is a pastor, student, cat-lover (which is my favorite trait), God fearing man, and a gifted writer. His unique writing and storytelling style is so captivating. We met at a local restaurant and immediately had a connection. For the first time in a very long time, I felt both seen and understood. We poured out our story and journey to him over lunch. He listened intently and anticipated the reader's questions in the brilliant way he crafted the article. His tongue-in-cheek style, quirky undertones, and brilliant witty sarcasm made for the perfect feature in *Oklahoman.com*.

The article was titled, "Innovative Oklahoma City Keller Williams sales team uses humor to push home sales." One of my favorite quotes from the article was "Our marketing may seem out of the box, quirky, fun-spirited, but make no mistake, this team gets results and performs at a high level and will continue to dominate the market."

This connection and relationship has grown even fonder over the last seven years. Don't ever underestimate the power of someone believing in you and offering you exposure. Richard has contributed so much to our careers, commanding name recognition and a tailored branding to our business. It is a relationship we still cherish to this day.

Keller Williams Realty agents Troy and Denise Schroder have become known for their quirky marketing.

Oklahoma City real estate sales team uses humor to sell homes

BY RICHARD MIZE
Real Estate Editor
richardmize@oklahoman.com

THERE Troy and Denise Schroder are, stuffed into a shirt as big as a tent and one huge pair of pants.

The photo is a marketing ploy: Their sales team at Keller Williams Realty is "getting too big for our britches!" (Insert groan here).

There they are again — he with a certain superhero's familiar "S" busting out of his button-down business shirt and tie, and her in a full Supergirl costume.

Why? Because this "looks like a job for ... the Schroder Group: Aggressive, Passionate, Relentless." (Oh, boy.)

There they are yet again — Troy, 47, with magician's wand, topcoat and stovepipe hat, Denise, 42, dressed to the nines as a magician's assistant holding a "SOLD" sign. (Eye rolling is occurring.)

So is chortling, snickering and giggling — but the Schroders, who lead the Schroder Team at Keller Williams Elite, 5629 N Classen Blvd., are the ones laughing all the way to success.

Because there Denise Schroder was on a marketing panel at Keller Williams Realty's annual "Family Reunion," where some 10,000 real estate agents gathered in Phoenix in 2014, not much more than a year after she got her real estate license.

And there the Schroders were late last year on HGTV's hit series "House Hunters" for the show's first stop in Oklahoma City. "House Hunters" takes viewers behind the scenes as home shoppers make emotional decisions that go with finding and buying a home.

They will be on a return episode — as soon as they find the right "camera-ready" buyer.

Who's groaning, oh-boying and eye-rolling now? Probably the same people who are attaboying the couple as they stake out the contours of a midlife dream.

"I was 39 and Troy was 44 years old before we found our 'calling,' " Denise Schroder said.

She said she'd wanted to become a Realtor 22 years ago when she worked in property management as a successful leasing agent. Then she became a stay-at-home mom before going back to work.

Troy Schroder was a Realtor for "one short year" while working a full-time job. He sold seven houses that year, balancing home sales with a job as a FedEx driver — sometimes changing from his FedEx uniform into a suit and tie, in the truck, to get to appointments right after work.

A year of that was enough.

Everything changed in 2010, when Troy and Denise got married and "blended five teenagers." That December, with money saved, they quit their jobs and took the plunge into owning their own business as real estate agents.

"We had many naysayers, but failure was not an option. We have never looked back! ... We jumped in with both feet and we decided to be truly 'authentic,' " Denise Schroder said. "By using my gift and extreme passion in marketing and creativity, we could be top of mind when you think of a ... Realtor. We are so passionate, relentless, driven, loyal, expeditious, dedicated, and get results."

In the first year,

> OUR MARKETING MAY SEEM OUT OF THE BOX, QUIRKY, FUN-SPIRITED, BUT MAKE NO MISTAKE, THIS TEAM GETS RESULTS AND PERFORMS AT A HIGH LEVEL AND WILL CONTINUE TO DOMINATE THE MARKET.
>
> DENISE SCHRODER

she said, they reached their goal of being in the Top 10 in their Keller Williams operation and in the top 3 percent in production among the 3,800 Realtors in the Oklahoma City metro area. They have maintained that level, she said.

All while being quirky. Goofy, even.

"Our marketing may seem out of the box, quirky, fun-spirited, but make no mistake, this team gets results and performs at a high level and will continue to dominate the market," she said.

Growth by word of mouth is the aim — or, "referral based," as it's put in business speak.

"We can hoot and holler all day about our accomplishments and how fast our business has catapulted and the level it has been blessed by God. What truly matters is what our clients take from the job we have done and the relationship we have built that will sustain the test of time," Denise Schroder said.

About all the laughs?

"Real estate transactions can be stressful. They are major life changes. When we can capture pockets of laughter and happiness, we do it. We don't take ourselves too seriously in that respect," she said.

"We also find great joy in helping others build their businesses. For example, our lender, inspectors, handymen, appliance repair, CPA, etc. are our business partners, and we believe in a high level of reciprocation and 'paying it forward.' We want our clients to get superb customer service (from) anyone we refer — to in essence be an extension of our business."

So, the Schroders are after more than just laughs and their hijinks. They're after genuine smiles, too.

85th ANNIVERSARY

INNOVATOR ARTICLE BY RICHARD MIZE

228

I am like a toddler, if you tell me I can't do something, I will show YOU. This behavioral trait was born in my after I had been painted by someone else as being too crippled to be bold and brave. It is a good and bad trait to have for sure. Being in the real estate world, my next goal was to get published in *Inman News*. *Inman* describes itself on its website as, "Inman is known for its award-winning journalism, cutting-edge technology coverage, in-depth educational opportunities, and forward-thinking events. *Inman* is the industry's leading source of real estate information." In a nutshell, *Inman News* is the pinnacle of where I wanted to be validated and published. Several people discouraged me when I mentioned it, saying it was too hard to get submissions published. So, that was my next conquest.

I reached out and sent an email with our bio, story, and resume. I expected to receive an autoreply thanking me for the submission and then be politely ghosted. I received an email back from a writer for *Inman* rather quickly. She wanted to do a Q and A on our Innovative marketing approach. I was thrilled and shocked! Relentless pursuit and consistent perseverance are all it takes to achieve the unthinkable. If your goals don't make you sweat, go back to the drawing board. If you are surrounded by nay-sayers who try to hold you back rather than help propel you, get new friends and a new sphere of influence. If I had listened to all the negative noise around me, it would have robbed me of an incredible opportunity. Please hear me when I say this, be fiercely intentional about who pours into your life.

A couple of my favorite takeaway quotes from the publication were these:

Would you spin a sign to sell a listing?

Denise and Troy Schroder would. In fact, they used "human signage" to direct traffic to an Open House. They were the fourth agent or agent group to try to sell this home, they said, and by the end of the event, the signage won them eight new leads.

"I have always been very creative," Denise Schroder said. "We used to own a photography company, so in my eyes, everything is a 'photo op.'" The Schroders even incorporate fun photo props into their clients' closing celebration photos.

NO SMOKE AND MIRRORS HERE, THEY ARE EXCITED TO
CLOSE ON THEIR NEW HOME!

IF THERE IS AN OPPORTUNITY TO CELEBRATE WITH
CONFETTI & TUTUS, WE WILL FIND IT!

CLOSING CELEBRATION PICS

Alby said in one of our most beautiful testimonial videos that we have a way of making people feel special. That, my friend, is what it is all about. Drop the mic....

These examples are just a few surreal achievements from published pieces. The magnitude of gratitude for the FREE exposure is mind boggling. It represents a journalist seeing something in us and being so inspired by our differentiation and our story they want to share it with the world! We set out to show a story in how we market and share experiences and testimonials. It all comes back to story-showing.

CHOSEN FOR THE COVER OF REAL PRODUCERS

REAL PRODUCERS COVER

THE OKLAHOMAN | OKLAHOMAN.COM Saturday, August 24

REALESTATE + HOME & GARDEN

Camera operator Chris McCaffrey records Oklahoma City real estate agents Troy and Denise Schroder for their third appearance on HGTV's "House Hunters." [PHOTOS PROVIDED]

For the third time charmed

Real estate couple star on HGTV again, and again, and again

Denise Schroder is recorded walking down stairs for an episode of "House Hunters."

The first time was a charm, in 2014. The second time was a charm, in 2017.

The third time, in 2019, makes enough for a bracelet.

Troy and Denise Schroder, real estate agents with Keller Williams Realty Elite, 5820 N Classen Blvd., will star in "House Hunters" on HGTV for the third time at 9 p.m. Thursday.

Denise told the unlikely story from the beginning this week in an email interview.

Q. What? You did it again? Remind us: How did this thing between you all and HGTV get started in the first place?

Denise: I spoke at a Keller Williams National Convention on marketing in Phoenix, Arizona, in 2013. I was approached after speaking on the panel by an agent that had previously been on "House Hunters" herself and she thought

Richard Mize

I would be great on the show. I contacted the casting department and imagine this: I was persistent, LOL! Oklahoma is obviously not a coastal and not exactly on their hit list of regular states to film. However, I sent them a link that the LA Times had recently written on how awesome our city is. We auditioned and the next thing you know HGTV was coming to OKC!

Q. Isn't it unusual for "House Hunters" to come back to the same city, with the same people (you and Troy), twice, let alone three times? What are y'all doing to make it happen?

Denise: It does seem unusual but I am so thankful that they think we are

See **CHARMED**, B2

HYDRATE YOUR GARDEN
In the scorching August heat, watering is job No. 1

BELLE ISLE BEAUTY
This midcentury home in the Belle Isle neighborhood has been redesigned with an open floor plan

'FutureHAUS' brings tomorrow's home into today's world

By Nina Zafar
The Washington Post

Innovation in digital technologies has transformed the way we live, with advances in smartphones, robotics and computers revolutionizing every aspect of our lives, yet these technologies remain object focused vs. concept focused.

At Virginia Tech, an interdisciplinary team of 25 students and faculty is taking existing technologies that work independently of one other and asking the question, why can't these components work together? Their FutureHAUS

project is about creating an interface that is completely connected within one smart-home system.

Virginia Tech placed first in Dubai's Solar Decathlon Middle East competition that challenged 15 universities from around the world to design, build and operate energy-positive solar homes. While the baseline for the competition revolved around energy efficiency within a 900-square-foot space, what differentiated FutureHAUS from its competitors was the smart technologies.

See **FUTURE**, B2

The FutureHAUS designed by Virginia Tech connects a house full of smart-home technologies through a single interface. [VIRGINIA TECH/THE WASHINGTON POST]

HGTV, HOUSE HUNTERS COVER PAGE ARTICLE

DENISE FAWN SCHRODER

Denise and Troy Schroder

AGENT ADVICE (HTTP://WWW.INMAN.COM/CATEGORY/AGENT-ADVICE/),
BRANDING (HTTP://WWW.INMAN.COM/CATEGORY/BRANDING-2/), CONTENT
MARKETING (HTTP://WWW.INMAN.COM/CATEGORY/CONTENT-MARKETING-2/)

Q&A: Denise and Troy Schroder, OKC's 'Innovators of the Year' and 'House Hunters' guest stars

These newer agents have radical marketing and retention ideas that have brought them success

by Rachael Hite (http://www.inman.com/author/rachael-hite/)

(mailTo:rachaelhite@gmail.com)   (https://www.twitter.com/rachaelhite)   May 20, 2015

INMAN NEWS ARTICLE

REAL ESTATE TOP PRODUCER MAGAZINE

Chapter 27
Podcast Guesting

"Despite criticisms of why podcasting won't work, the facts tell a different story. According to Edison Research, the number of Americans who listen to a podcast each week has grown 100% over the past four years. In fact, one hundred million Americans listen to a podcast every month."

According to Buzzsprout, here is the dish:

Podcasting has grown drastically and steadily since it began in the early 2000s.

The industry grew alongside the advent of smartphones, smart speakers (Amazon Alexa, Google Home, etc.), and in-dash entertainment systems.

- In 2022, 51% of the population has listened to a podcast and roughly 78% are familiar with the medium.

- Podcast listeners increased by 29.5% from 2018 to 2021.

- Over one-third (104 million) of Americans listen to podcasts regularly.

- According to Edison Research, 41% (116 million) listened to a podcast in the last month.

- 28% (80 million) of Americans are weekly podcast listeners.

One of my focuses for 2020 was to do podcast guesting. And yes, "guesting" is an actual word. It is a verb! You can google it if you don't believe me! I have spoken about it a little bit earlier, but I wanted to dive in a little deeper. With podcasts being all the rage, this is a content marketing strategy that can yield big results. My goal was to be featured on one podcast a week. For the first two months, I was strategically lasering in on it, my average was two a week.

I sat down and mapped out what my WHY is in pursuing podcast guesting. One of my WHYs is to polish and perfect my public speaking skills. The other WHY that is more motivational than any other reason is I know I have a story and message to tell that will inspire others. It is that simple. By the way, your story and testimony does not have to be as dramatic as a Lifetime movie script or a Jerry Springer episode to be entertaining and gripping. Don't overcomplicate this or you will start listening to your devil on your shoulder and never get off the bench.

Podcast guests are so powerful. Podcast audiences are on the rise every day. Being on podcasts is also a wonderful way to refine your public speaking skills. With little preparation, once your story is polished, you can gain new engagement and a large audience of fresh, prospective customers. I started researching Facebook groups, which is a tool many people underestimate. I summarized my story, created my speaker one-sheet, and had a creative marketing photo that stopped everyone's scroll. My photo I include is me wearing my wedding dress in front of a home with the caption "You'll love this house so much you'll Want to marry it!" (There is a story about this dress and This gorgeous Victorian home in the background, you will hear about it later.)

I designed a speaker one-sheet on Canva. This is a simple one-page document detailing the basic topics you can present, your unique expertise, and your contact details. I began posting it on Facebook groups where podcast speakers were being requested. I posted this speaker one-sheet in the Public Speaking chapter. I was surprisingly flooded with responses about having me as a guest on their show. An invitation to be a guest is gold! You have access to anywhere from hundreds to thousands of committed listeners. One of the amazing benefits is you get to be published on the host's blog with links via a show notes page. Not to mention all their social media platform blasts they push out. Some hosts provide a transcript of the interview. If they don't, you can ask permission to do this, and a transcription service is very reasonable. Embedding a podcast audio file on your website is really beneficial. Many SEO experts say that Google ratings are based on sites rankings and the amount of time actually spent. For a consumer to be watching the twenty to forty-minute podcast on your site may help your SEO efforts.

DENISE SCHRODER

SCHRODER REAL ESTATE GROUP/OKLAHOMA

Realtor, CEO, Speaker, Author, Marketing Strategist

AS SEEN ON

CONNECT WITH ME:

WWW.FACEBOOK.COM/TDSCHRODER

INSTAGRAM:@DENISESELLSOKLAHOMA

SCHRODERGROUPLLC@GMAIL.COM

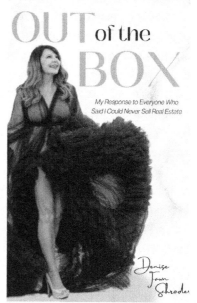

OUT of the BOX

My Response to Everyone Who Said I Could Never Sell Real Estate

HGTV

SPEECH TOPICS:

HOW TO GO FROM BROKEN TO BARRIER BREAKER

STEPPING OUT OF THE BOX AND PAVING YOUR OWN LANE

HOW TO TURN YOUR PAIN INTO PURPOSE

SPEAKER ONE SHEET EXAMPLE

Podcast guesting gives you an added sense of credibility. It is such an influential way you can be introduced to a loyal following that trusts the host's judgment and recommendations implicitly.

Once you get really polished telling your story and your message, level up! I am always pushing and challenging myself to go bigger. Ask for a few people you trust to give you constructive feedback and share the notes with you. You have to give others the permission to be brutally honest. Many habits we have in public speaking and things we say in our normal vernacular may not be good. I was schooled and empowered in my initial public speaking skills through pageants. I was taught that "umm" is a dirty word. It is one of the number one things I try to avoid saying. If I have an answer I need to think about, I take a breath and a brief pause. Find podcasts that you enjoy listening to and that have an audience whose attention you want to capture and ultimately reach! Research the podcast's brand and really ensure the conversations they are having are like-minded with what you stand for personally and professionally. You need to listen to several episodes and be familiar with their topics and structure. Also, research the podcaster on a deeper level. Seek out their website and social media presence to really get a feel for what they represent. You can also easily engage with them on their social media accounts as well as share their content. Comment and have conversations on their Twitter, for example, which may anchor your name in their mind when they receive a pitch from you. When you write your guest pitch, connect with the host in a unique and creative way. You can find something you are both passionate about from your research and mention it in your pitch. Remember, social media creeping is a great way to get an idea of who someone is, their interests, hobbies, and personality. Taking assiduous notes while you are doing your homework on each show is imperative. Highlight and flag powerful takeaways from the episodes you listened to and reference those in your pitch. This shows the host you were inspired, have a genuine interest in their podcast, and in them as a person. The main objective is to communicate how your message will extend massive value to their audience. Period. What can your interview do to impact the listeners in a profound way that makes the host look great!

After you do the podcast, follow up with an email asking them for a review of you as a guest. You can compile many to use as references for future guest opportunities or speaking gigs for more added credibility. You should also review their podcast immediately on multiple platforms where they are available. You love reviews for your business, so always, always reciprocate at a high level and follow through with your promises. Ultimately, people want to help one another. Cross-promoting is a beautiful gift to each party. Communicate from the beginning that you will give them glowing reviews and you would like one as well, and express your gratitude in advance.

When you are pitching yourself as a guest, highlight that you will be promoting, boosting, blasting out to your entire large database on all your social media platforms. Let the host or booking agent know how strongly you feel about building new listeners through you being a guest on the show. It is about THEM, not you! Your message to the podcast host is always, "How can I help your podcast?"

You should also provide links to other podcasts you have done. This really gives the host/booking agent a tangible example of how you represent as a guest.

When I have done podcasts, they are typically Zoom calls. The podcast is usually just audio, so I was confused at first why we had to do a face-to-face video. Until now, I have done both, on the phone only or Zoom. You can truly connect with the host on a deeper level than simply a phone conversation. Being able to have eye contact, see someone smile, or read their body language is just huge when you are spilling your guts to a mere stranger. I have developed friendships with many of these powerhouse, lifegiving women. They are in my newsfeed, and I take a daily opportunity to cheer them on and interact on their pages in order to edify them. These hosts have become women I can call on when I need advice. I know they are genuinely happy to help if I reach out my hand. I have been astounded at the bond I have been able to build with these hosts from an intake and a forty-minute to hourlong conversation. The conversation is just beginning after we have connected on a more deep-seated level.

I am including brief excerpts from the show notes for the blog that Jared Orton of *Bananas for Business* posted after our podcast. As you read through the show notes after you do a guest spot, it is so fulfilling to hear from the host's perspective what their takeaways were from your story. Some of them surprised me and I realized different chords that were struck so I know to dig deeper on those points moving forward because they were possibly more impactful than I anticipated. The show notes are a detailed form of feedback of your interview and how your story and message was perceived. This is powerful!

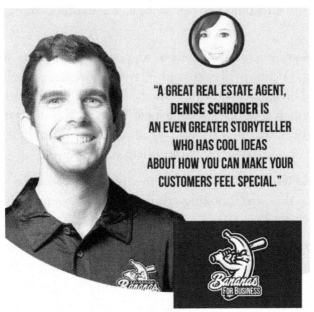

BANANAS FOR BUSINESS PODCAST PROMO
WITH JARED ORTON

BANANAS FOR BUSINESS PODCAST PROMO WITH JARED
ORTON

From the podcast, Bananas for Business by Jared Orton

The way you treat your customers constantly cycles back to the returns you receive from the loyalty you've worked for. Making customers feel special will put them in a mindset and position where they feel great about their work with you and give them the inclination to recommend you to their loved ones, and those referrals, in turn, go to you and create new business—and so on. Denise Schroder is one half of the Schroder Real Estate Group, working together with her husband Troy. Jared Orton interviews Denise about the "Red Carpet Treatment" her business rolls out for their most loyal customers, which ends up drumming up more business for her company. The saying goes, "What goes around comes around," and it's no different when you're doing business, so learn what you could be doing today.

—Jared Orton

To inspire people, don't show them your super powers. Show them theirs.

Alexander den Heijer

"Learning And Telling Your Customers' Story with Denise Schroder"

Thanks for reading this episode. I've got a ridiculously fun conversation to bring to you with Denise Schroder. Denise has become a friend of the Bananas and a friend of this show for a little while now. I heard her story and found out everything that she went through to get to this point of being a remarkable real estate agent in the Oklahoma City area. I was like, "We have got to record this out and get this to people." Some amazing things are going on with Denise and her husband, Troy. What they're doing for their people in the Oklahoma City market is so much fun. It is exciting. It had me laughing. It had me writing down ideas and sharing them with our team. I was like, "This is fun."

I don't know if I've heard of real estate agents having this much fun and doing these cool things for people like Troy and Denise are doing. What I'll preface this with is that what I realized early on and what Denise realized early on is she has the gift of storytelling. She might be a real estate agent, but her power is telling her story. Not only that but also telling the story of her clients and customers and realizing that has become the calling card for putting their message out about how they could connect with people. As we've said over and over again, people do business with people. You're going to find that with my conversation with Denise. It's absolutely funny and amazing. There are cool ideas that you'll learn at the end of this story. You'll be like, "I've got to take that back to my team, my business, and my customers. Here's my conversation with Denise Schroder.

—

JO: Denise, how is it going? I am pumped to have you and have this conversation.

DS: I am more excited than you know. When I got the email about this conversation, I screamed, "I'm going to be on a Bananas interview. What are you talking about?"

JO: This is Bananas for Business, and we are having these types of conversations with people who are doing things dramatically different. When I heard your story and your husband's story, where all this has come from and where it is now, it was a no-brainer that we had to share what's going on in Oklahoma City with people. If we were to travel to Oklahoma City, what is the one thing that we've had to do there that you always recommend people doing?

DS: Our downtown is incredible. We have a brick town. We have tons of live music entertainment. If you're a foodie, this is the place to be. We've got many new restaurants. We have the Oklahoma City Thunder, which is a huge draw. Our city has grown so much that people haven't been here in a decade or so, it's unrecognizable. We've grown so much. If you ever come to Oklahoma City, I'll get my car wrapped in bananas. We'll paint the town. There are a lot of people here.

JO: Are you from that area originally or did you guys move there? What's your backstory in the market in general?

DS: I am a small-town farmer's daughter from a little town by the border of Kansas. I moved to the Oklahoma City area in 1993. I've been here for a long time. I've got a sphere of influence here now.

JO: You've had this passion for real estate for a long time, but it took you twenty-plus years to get into it. Talk to us about that. You're from a small town, you're moving to Oklahoma City, and you want to be in real estate. Give us some of that backstory. Where did all this come from? What was it like as you were starting to try to figure out what you were trying to do and what your purpose was in those early stages of your career?

DS: Many years ago, I worked in property management. I was what you call a floater. I had some high success where I would go around and I would get the occupancy rates up because I was their "closer." I enjoyed doing that and I enjoyed helping people find a place they're going to call home. Everybody around me, my bosses and coworkers said, "The natural progression for you is real estate. This is going to get monotonous to you. You need to get your license." Unfortunately, I was surrounded by some people in my personal life that told me I could never make it, couldn't stand out and we weren't going to lie in the garage with vein metal signs with my pictures on them. That wasn't going to happen. I shelved it or suppressed it for over twenty years.

JO: Why were people saying that? Was it a market thing? Was it a you thing? Where was that negativity coming from for someone saying that you weren't going to succeed in real estate?

DS: Oklahoma City has grown so much in the span of one decade thanks to the many things it has to offer.

It always has been saturated. There are thousands of realtors in our marketplace. We're in the top 50. I think that sometimes when other people don't have dreams, they want to steal yours. In my situation, I was in a relationship where I was put in someone else's box, and I allowed that to happen. It's a big learning lesson for me and one that I'm thankful for.

JO: Twenty years of thinking, you know you want to be in real estate. What were you doing in those twenty-plus years? What was life like for Denise at that time?

DS: I feel like I've lived a lot of lifetimes but I'm not going to tell you how old I am. I've been an OB-GYN surgical tech, a personal trainer, an admin assistant. I owned a company. I moved to a different suburb. To back up, I went through a very acrimonious divorce and custody battle that cost me about $50,000. It was a dark period of my time fighting for my wealth, my kids and what was best. In the midst of that, I lost my mother. She got misdiagnosed with a hernia and had colon cancer. That was a difficult time where I developed my grit. I was in survival mode. I got through the next several years. I'm taking care of my kids. That was my main focus. It wasn't me. When I moved to this little suburb, I was working in a high school office. I was an admin assistant to several principals and in walks my FedEx guy. I always tell him he has a Julia Roberts-like smile.

JO: What a manly thing to say.

DS: He had the sexiest legs and I saw him every day for about five years before our first date. I tried to set him up with other people. I wasn't in a position. I wasn't ready to be in a relationship, but he was a great guy. I even tried to set him up with some of my friends at school where I worked, but that didn't work out thankfully. We had our first date and six months later we're married. We've blended five teenagers. Ten months later, we both quit our jobs on the same day, both with salary jobs and great benefits. We took a leap. It was extremely scary because I'm a woman and I like security. I like to know that everything's going to be taken care of, that we got an emergency fund and all that. It was betting the farm type behavior for me.

JO: I feel like people reading this are like, "What in the world?" You have someone who has done every job under the sun, who's a high school admin person. You have a FedEx driver, they blend their families, get married and then ten months later quit their jobs. What's next? I feel like I'm crafting a reality TV show. What made you all say, "Quit our jobs now, we're going to launch ourselves into this real estate career?" Jesse used the term "mirror moment" a lot. What was that mirror moment for you where you said, "We're to go in this way, we're taking a 180, we're going in a different direction and we're going to leap all in?"

DS: We had a childhood friend of Troy's that was a mentor to him. He was doing financial services and that was Troy's dream. I was along for the ride. I said, "I'll get my license. We'll start a business together." Shortly after we quit our jobs, we realized this gentleman was going bankrupt. He was not doing well in his finances.

JO: Getting finance advice from someone who's been bankrupt.

DS: That was a blow. We did several different things before we finally got to real estate. We didn't have our first transaction until 2013. For three years we refused to go back, get a job and work for the man. We had so many people that thought we were crazy and nut bags. We were not going to fail. We were doing jobs that we weren't even telling our family or our children about. We're going door to door selling roofs. In Oklahoma, roofs get totaled a lot. We were doing things under the radar because we weren't going to quit. We were going to do whatever it took until we figured out what our calling. I knew what my calling was. When Troy said, "Let's get our real estate licenses," it was like angels were singing. That's how that began. It was like we're going to do this differently and I'm going to be unapologetically myself, which is weird and creative. I used to have a photography business too. That plays a big role in my creativity.

JO: Something interesting that I heard there, and I want people to always understand this, is this was not an overnight success for you where you guys said, "We're getting our real estate license tomorrow and now we've sold one billion houses so far." It took you three years of methodically grinding through, working through, finding your purpose, finding your place, serving others, taking care of others, putting your family first to get to that point of, "Now the light bulb turns on. We want to be in real estate, and we want to make that jump." I hope I'm saying that right. This was not an overnight success.

DS: It took us seven months once we got our licenses that we even received a paycheck. We were living off of $30,000 in savings, which seems nuts when I look back if that's what we had. I was like, "We'll never have to dip into it because we're going to be successful." That was mind-boggling to us. That keeps depleting and your kids need braces, or someone gets a flat tire. Everything was a struggle. Seven months, no paycheck. As I said earlier, I'm a farmer's daughter. My dad was one of the few people that 100% said when we called him and said we're going to become self-employed. He's never worked for the man. He graduated from college with an Ag degree. He has run this family business for 50 years, and he said, "Go do it. Plant your seeds, plow, sow, and harvest." Whenever I'd call and say, "Still nothing, dad. We're door knocking, we're doing open houses, we're cold calling everyone, nothing's happening. Am I not doing what I'm supposed to be doing? I thought this was my calling." He said, "It'll come to fruition. You have to be patient." In the last five months of that first year, we sold 40 houses. We couldn't even keep up with ourselves because it all came popping up at once.

JO: Making Customers Feel Special: When other people don't have dreams, they want to steal yours. If you're in a situation wherein you're in someone else's box, you're inclined to allow that to happen.

JO: At that time, I assume you had to work probably underneath someone else's brokerage as you were getting your feet wet.

DS: We're under Keller Williams brokerage. I don't want my own brokerage because I didn't want to be responsible if you go out and get a lawsuit.

JO: You two were working on your own at that point. I didn't know if you were a part of someone else's team or someone else's group or anything like that. Talk about those first seven months. You were sharing it right there. It sounded like you were doing everything that everyone else was doing. You were doing open houses, cold calling, knocking on doors and putting out signs. Where did the transition come from where you put all that work in seven months? Did you make a big change that's flipped the switch for you?

DS: We went to every educational class known to man because I wanted to be as confident. I'm handling people's largest investments. I took that very seriously. He was the FedEx guy in town for fifteen years. Everyone still had him branded as, "I'm going to let the FedEx guy."

JO: It's not quite the brand marketing you're looking for.

DS: We were reinventing ourselves together as a team. We did a couple of things. I had been on Oprah many years ago and she told me, "You have a gift of storytelling."

JO: Go into that a little bit. I'm interested in this.

DS: I wrote to her after I had my second child. I won't go into all the details. They called us and flew up to our house. The producer filmed us for about eight hours, built our story and then they flew us out. I thought I was going to be in the front row. She said, "I want her on stage with me the entire show." I'm like deer in the headlights, "What?" We're there. It was a big women's issue. That was one of the highly rated shows in 1999. We went back for a follow-up show. Before the show started, she said, "Denise, you and I are in my living room. We're having a conversation. The reason why you're here is because you're transparent and you can show a story." I remember her saying that to me and I thought, "Oprah Winfrey told me I know how to show a story." I felt completely at ease. She stood up, unbuttoned her top button, and said, "We're in my living room." I remember it changing my life in a way that tells the story. That's how I've chronicled my business and everything creative I've ever done. It's about telling a story.

JO: That is fascinating because many times as businesses, we're trying to advertise and sell. People want to be told a story. They want to feel like they're a part of something. We're all human. Humans do business with humans. We don't want to be sold some big marketing plan like, "Get in front of me and talk to me like I'm in my living room." That is fascinating to me. How has that changed your entire mindset of being an agent and working with people? Keep going a little bit on that storytelling piece. I think that's fascinating.

DS: We were trying to rebrand ourselves as real estate agents. We had blended these five crazy teenagers. I had gotten an email from the Steve Harvey Show, and I sent a video back. We were asked to be blended family experts and talk about the dangers of teen technology, which I am an expert in. Anyone who wants to know what apps children can't have, call me. He introduced us as Troy and Denise Schroder, real estate agents from Oklahoma City. I started using that snippet in my promos. Who has Steve Harvey introduced them for anything, anywhere or anytime in their life? I started using that online and people are like, "They're on major TV shows." Shortly after that, we got on HGTV, which has never been to Oklahoma City, and they thought we were rednecks.

JO: I'd be amazed to know they think we are.

DS: They didn't want to come here but we pitched them. They came and we've been invited back two times since. I think that show gets to about 90 million households. Early on, we were developing a brand and a recognizable name in the industry, and we were selling. At that point, we had gotten through our first year. We're rock and rolling but the TV presence, all the human story press releases, all the things around these TV opportunities I was having on The Talk and Rachel Ray, I'm doing something on another network that's going to be out in a few months. All things go back to real estate. When they play this show, I'm getting ready to be on, when they put my name on the screen, they put "real estate agent" underneath it. I always want all these things I do to come back to what I do.

JO: It's interesting that you're a real estate agent, but you see yourself as a storyteller and someone who's continually sharing, "I do sell homes. I do sell real estate. I can help you out by doing this but I'm a great storyteller." How does someone who maybe hasn't gotten access to big media channels potentially start becoming a storyteller in their business? What type of suggestions would you give someone to say, "Here's how you start telling your story?"

DS: It's simple because I feel like if you are coming with your clients with a genuine open heart, you make them comfortable. I feel like everybody has a story and I love that. It's not about me. I love love stories, but it's not always love. Sometimes it's divorce and sometimes it's death. I ask people to tell me why they came to us and what their needs are. Even if they don't tell me because I'm in such an intimate relationship with them, I earned the right to ask them relational personal questions. I will say, "I love your story. Will you please share it with me?" I don't want it commercialized. I don't want it to be professional. I want it to be, "You and I are having a conversation. I want you to tell me your story. Why are we here now?" They'll say, "We're selling our family home. My parents got engaged on the driveway and it's been in our family for fifty years," and they're crying. I'm melting because I'm a sincere emotional person. I love those kinds of videos more than, "She sold my house in one day." I'd rather have the story of who they are.

If anyone can take anything away from this, it's how we are asking for the stories of our customers so that they stop becoming transactional and they start becoming human. We can understand why we're serving. You can sell and buy houses all day long and you can run them up and down, but you take the time to understand the why behind the buy or the sell. What you're saying is that it gives you so much credibility and power in that relationship that they'll trust you with anything.

We've sold 500 homes in seven years and so we have credibility. Where the mind switch came to me was because I waited long to start my career. I felt like I had to play catch up because I'm now starting my career. I'm almost 40, my life's almost over. You know how women feel when they're almost 40. My mom died at 50. I had a perspective that changed me in a way that I can't explain. When people say they live like they're dying. I do because I saw a bucket list that my mom never got to fulfill and thought she had all the time in the world to do. I look at things a little bit differently than most people.

You have to earn the right with people to ask them to share their stories. If you are relational in your business, they know that and they feel that. They know you care about them. You can't just, "You bought something from me," and you're going to knock on their door, put some lipstick on it and do a story. You've got to have the relationships. You've got to go back to the foundation of are you taking the time to build the relationship? Is your business about the people and not about the ROI or what they can do for you or if you do this testimonial, it'll get me this? It all has to come from what is it? It's about you, not me.

We get a lot of questions like, "What's the ROI on creating this experience for someone?" You can't put an actual dollar figure on it, but we know in our heart of hearts that by delivering something for a person rather than just a product, it allows them to feel like they were in it for me, the customer. They weren't in it for the commission, or they got to hit that next benchmark, they were in it for me. You were talking about how you sold 500 homes and all those things. What is the relationship like after the sale or after the transaction is done? We struggle with this in our business. We haven't done a great job of continuing that relationship. How have you continued that relationship after technically your job is done?

It's my favorite part, honestly. I feel like it's my forte. I'm the director of woo is what I call myself because I'm courting these people. I'm trying to gain love and favor from our people. I'm trying to build relationships. After the transaction, we have a thing called the Red Carpet Club. My vision from the very beginning of our business and our branding has always been a red carpet. This is something that I was thinking about since I had emailed you. It's how you are as a person. We roll out the red-carpet treatment for customers. We want them to feel like royalty. In most of our events, we have them coming down the red carpet. We have them getting professionally photographed. As I've heard Jesse say, "It's about making them feel like they're famous." I hired photographers and videographers. We make them feel like they're so special.

When we have company over to our house, I've always done the red carpet for just my friends. If you stay the night at my house, you get mints and a handwritten card.

There are special things that we do for people in our personal life. I feel like if you're that way in your personal life, this is an extension of who I am. The people aren't my clients, they're my tribe, they're my family. We're doing life together. One thing that made me realize that we have a relationship-focused business almost 100% is when you are asked to sing at funerals of your clients' parents and sing at weddings. We get invited to all their showers, weddings, baby,

253

gender reveals. We're doing life with them. It's not forced, it's a relationship. Afterwards, we have a Red Carpet Club. We do monthly giveaways. It's about you, giving away different prizes. We do dance and dashes. We started doing this. If you win one of the giveaways and they're cool giveaways, I'm going to show up at your door. Statistically, you'll have a ring doorbell and if you don't, I want to buy you one.

JO: Denise will install one for you, so you can get the giveaway.

DS: We started doing this around Christmas time. We were whipping and nae-naeing at everyone's door and leaving them their little gift. People were posting them everywhere. We've shown up at grocery stores as superheroes. For celebratory things during mapping our experience, I make Troy do this, I don't even know how he doesn't leave me. Have you ever heard a lullaby being played over the intercom when new babies are born at hospitals? This is my skewed version of that! Troy gets dressed up with me in a Spartan cheerleader outfit. We'll literally cheer about appraisals being met and things that are exciting to the client. We do this every day. It doesn't excite us that much, but it's the biggest deal to them, so it's the biggest deal to me. I'm going to make sure they understand we're celebrating with them.

JO: Making Customers Feel Special: Roll out the "Red Carpet Treatment" for your customers. You want your customers to feel like they're famous, like they're royalty.

JO: I love all these cheerleading appraisals and dancing dash. I've never heard that in my life. The question we get a lot is like, "Real estate is serious. It's supposed to be buttoned up. You're supposed to be in a shirt and tie. This is a $1 million investment. How can you be non-serious?" You guys are having fun. How do you share that message with somebody who would ask you that question like, "Aren't we supposed to be serious?" How do you answer that because these are absolutely fun?

DS: We've earned the right. At first, it was a little bit of a balancing act. That's not who I am. Let me handle finding you a home and helping you get top dollar. It's a different dynamic. We've earned the right and we have this perfect recipe where our audience and our clients especially know that when it's time to take care of business, they are the negotiators. They're expeditious. They communicate and serve as they've chosen at the highest level. You never have to worry about what's next and what's happening. They have it handled.

We've earned the right to inject that joy and fun because it's not always fun. There are a lot of bumps in real estate transactions. We deal with divorce and I'm talking dirty, messy, nasty divorces and deaths. We treat those differently, but we still bring happiness to people in an empathetic way. We take that seriously. We've got our Family Law mediator certificate because we deal with high-conflict resolution. We need those skills. We take everything we do seriously. I feel like we earned the right to inject that fun because people know with our results-oriented business, with us to prove that we do have a serious side.

JO: What you're saying is the dance and dash don't matter if you fumble the appraisal. You've got to get the main thing and you've earned that right. You've earned that trust. You are super highly experts in this industry and so you get to buy that. You get permission to inject this fun. I'm glad you mentioned the different experiences you provide because we all deal with different styles of customers. A first-time home buyer is different than, "My family member passed away and I'm selling their home." You said something powerful. You're always looking to inject happiness into that person's life. That might be a cheerleader video, or it might be, "We care for you." It might be, "We are thankful that you chose us to help you out." Go back to the Red Carpet Club. You always saw the business as this red carpet. Where did that come from? It's interesting that businesses need to define that experience mindset that they want to provide to their customers and clients. Where did this red-carpet mentality come from?

DS: The red-carpet mentality came from probably me being in music and theater. I've always performed. Whenever you're on the red carpet, there's something prestigious and special about it. I knew that I had so much fun. When my friends from high school would come over, I rolled the red carpet out and they loved it. It's all about the way you make people feel. I knew that I wanted to give a level of service that, as your organization and Jesse says, you're creating people to market for you. You don't have to market. What

I'm doing is I'm telling stories and I'm having fun. I might be stopping to scroll but I'm living in my organic truth and I'm having a blast.

JO: It comes down to, how do you make people feel? You've said some powerful words like love and happiness. Businesses don't use that very often about their customers and clients. When we create those emotions for customers and clients, they become fans. You have this Red Carpet Club. They're definitely fans. They go out and share, "I bought a house, and this is what they did for me."

DS: If it was your birthday and you got me dressed up in my Marilyn Monroe, the whole getup, the wigs, the diamonds, the mole and everything, I would send you a sing-a-gram. Would that be more meaningful and anchor with you more than posting on your wall, "HBD?"

JO: I'm pulling out my phone and I'm showing everyone around for the next two weeks, "Look what I got. These people are ridiculous." How did FedEx guy Troy respond to all this stuff? Where is he at in all this? You said he's dressing up as a cheerleader every once in a while, but what's his role? There are a lot of people who are dealing with, "Maybe it's a husband-and-wife team. Maybe I've got another partner in this." How is he as a business partner? Also, in the experience of the clients, where is he at in all this?

DS: He's amazing. He is so magnetic. He's an extrovert but he's more introvert than I am. He is very in-tune with client relationships. He calms everyone. I'm high energy, "Let's get it done." I'm a slave driver and he's reining me in. We bring a good balance to each other, but he's very much involved. Do I have to use my negotiating skills behind the scenes to get him to dress up sometimes? Yes, I do. After he does it and he sees how people respond to it, he is glad that we did it.

JO: You mentioned that one point right there. We're looking for those responses. Whether you have a two-person team, a ten-person team or however many people. If we get outside of our comfort zone a little bit and try something fun for someone. We see how they respond, and you get that joy and satisfaction of, "This worked." They smile, they laugh, and they show it to people. That's empowering to a team that you can say, "What if we did this for everyone? What if we did this for ten of our customers or twenty of our clients or however many? Let's keep this going because this feeling is powerful." Do you get that inside of you like, "We did this, what's next?"

DS: *We think we're doing things for other people, but we end up being rewarded more. To circle back to the Red Carpet Club post-transaction, we do high client events quarterly. One of the ones that I love the most and we get the best feedback is I'll have choices out in my backyard and in the beautiful backyard. We have a Victorian dollhouse. We live in a house that no one else has so it's different. People love coming over to the house and touring it and hanging out here. We'll do photo sessions for the families. I've even been a part of planning their engagements and being the photographer. I'm intimately involved with these people. They're asking me to help them plan proposals. It's crazy*

This is our latest idea and I'm excited. Angel Meyers was our first client. She couldn't sell her house for eighteen months to two different realtors. We had never sold a house. Our daughters were friends. They haven't been friends very long. We didn't have a relationship with her. She believed in us before anyone did and she hired us. We door knocked, did open houses and a broker's open. We sold her house and got multiple offers in one day. We didn't change the price. We helped her re-stage the home. We had a fierce conversation about having to clear things out a little bit, which was difficult. She's an interior designer. The house is beautiful but let's see more of the bones and it's sold. She has planted so many seeds in our business that I can't even retrace it all. We have implemented something and that's where I want all of the readers to know.

Every one of our clients, if they have a business that's like-minded where they serve the way we serve, we are asking them, "How can we help you build your business? What can we do?" We're promoting them, highlighting them, recommending them, doing videos about them, and promoting them in general. We came up with this idea where Angel is going to do a designer in a box. Two hours, $50, she shows up, hang pictures, moves furniture, she'll go with you to the shop and pick out things. This is a closing gift for realtors. This is a gift that anybody can give to anyone. We're doing something that no one else is doing. The reason why our clients are *loving it is that we're giving an experience. We're blessing her building this new branch of her business and we're blessing our clients because they are going crazy like, "I can't believe you gave me this." They think it's hundreds of dollars.*

JO: *The value in your mind is like, "I'm getting a private interior designer." We always use the term of, "I can't believe it. You wouldn't believe what I got." Traditionally, they put a champagne bottle or maybe a basket of things in your home when you walk in after the closing. To get experience and nobody else is doing this. Another thing you pointed out was you wanted to work with like-minded people who wanted to serve people in a way that you felt aligned. You're building their level of success. You're also building your client's level of success. That is powerful. I love that so much.*

DS: *One thing to remember too is I am sharing this with thousands of realtors in my marketplace. Even though I want to be different, I want to help them grow more than I care about myself and holding onto that as a secret.*

JO: *I have to imagine it comes back to you over and over. You said that you couldn't even trace the level of how much she shared that with people. That's an amazing idea. What else are you thinking about reimagining the client experience?*

DS: *We're doing weekly coffees and then we're doing this new thing that we haven't started yet. What we're going to do is we're going to draw out people in our Red Carpet Club, which are our top two hundred. We have 2,000 in our database. We can't be running and doing pop eyes to 2,000 people. It's not humanly possible. We can send mails out and different things, but we can't do some of the things that the core people that are referring to us actively, which are giving us a lot of business. We want to make sure we show them a high level of gratitude because they are feeding us and telling us they love us. We are going to do a thing called Schroder Smiles.*

You will get smiley faces. You're being flocked all over your yard. We're going to have a home-cooked meal delivered. You'll get to choose between three different meals and that's going to be delivered to you and your family. We're starting that and we're trying to do different and unexpected things. It's not during the holidays.

It's completely unexpected and we show up in these people's yards. We don't make it seem ritualistic or methodical like, "There's the monthly newsletter that's coming in." That's not us. We're going to do everything intentionally, but I don't want people to expect it.

There's a gray area there because it seems like, "I got the automated email, thank you, from them." There's also the side of like, "This could take all of our time and energy. We still have to sell homes. We can't always be event planners." There's that intentionality and also that thought process of how do we make it personal? How do we not take up all of our time doing this? You're doing this for a select group of people and that's okay. It's okay that everyone doesn't get this experience. They're going to get something else.

If they refer us to a client, they do get added to the club. There are some people that aren't interactive with you and that's okay.

JO: You've had a vast experience in your life. Where do you get all these ideas from? This is awesome. We feel like we come up with some creative ideas, but where do you get inspired? Where do these ideas come from? How are you cultivating these things? We get that question a lot, "How do you come up with ideas?" Where do you get yours from? How do you come up with them?

DS: I've always been a creative person. I feel like I drive people crazy around me. I'm voice texting ideas to myself in the middle of the night like. Troy was like, "What are you doing?" I'm like, "I've got to get this on my phone or I won't remember it in the morning." You think you'll remember it. If you put me in what I would call a think tank, I would love it. That's why I enjoy helping people build their businesses because I can come up with ideas for things easily. That's my gifting and I enjoy it. I would love to abandon Troy and come work for the Savannah Bananas because I would have the best time ever.

JO: Making Customers Feel Special: To anybody out there that's looking into recharging and resetting your business, surround yourself with a circle that cheers when you win.

JO: We'll bring you to one of our Ideapalooza sessions and let you run. You're coming up with ideas all the time, which is inspiring because that's where it takes some time to go. What's one that didn't work that you felt like, "This would've been so cool," and it fell flat on its face.

DS: We did one that I thought people would like. It morphed Troy's face and mine together. It made Troy look like me with facial hair on it and everything. I thought this is freaking hilarious. I was getting messages like, "That is creepy. Take that down." You never know when people are going to think it's weird or gross or offensive. I'm sure there have been many others that have flopped. There's one that you think will get a certain response and then you're like, "That didn't go over the way I thought it would. I thought people would find that was a lot funnier."

JO: I asked that question because I always want people to realize that even an idea that failed. It wasn't a failure. It just didn't work a little bit. You change, you do something different, you adapt, and you move. Nothing is truly a failure. It was an idea that didn't get the response you want. Sometimes we paralyze ourselves because we're like, "Will this idea work? Will people care?" Put it out there. Morph your faces together, see what happens and see if you get a response.

DS: It was a bad looking picture, apparently. Not everything works and that's okay. We pivot and keep going. To me, where I've learned the most things have been when things have gone wrong, when I've failed and when I've fallen. Those are the reasons why I come back better and stronger than before because I don't focus on them. I definitely learned from them. My rise-up muscles are strong, but coming from not focusing on all your fall downs because you're going to fall and you're going to fail and it's okay.

JO: Who are you learning from? Are you reading? Are you doing podcasts? I know you're out speaking and inspiring people, which is amazing. You're putting all this out there. You're helping build people. You're helping build people's businesses. You're giving so much to clients. How are you learning and developing? Where are you getting that from?

DS: I read a lot. I've read Raving Fans, which I loved and then Jesse's book. I listen to podcasts every day. I started listening to your podcast. I love Rachel Hollis. I listen to a lot of social media marketing. Because I've moved from production into purpose, which I've always had a purpose but I'm trying to figure out how real estate's a vehicle. It's allowing me to have more influence and impact because I've proven myself that I can speak and do these things that I didn't have the confidence to do before. I've been doing a lot of podcasts and I want to speak. I'm working on some out of the box marketing book and doing some things that are out of my comfort zone. Even though I can write a story, writing a book makes you feel naked.

I've never done this before. There are a lot of scary territories. To anybody out there that's looking into recharging and resetting your business or doing different things to amplify things, surround yourself with a circle that cheers when you win. They'll mourn and get on the floor with you when you're crying and help pull you up. I had to completely replenish my circle because I didn't have people around me that were challenging me. I had to give people permission to be transparent with me, not just to tell me what I want to hear, but to hold me accountable like coaches and mentors. I listen to podcasts all day every day while I'm working. If I'm not on the phone, I've got a podcast on. I'm a sponge.

JO: We always have to develop and evolve. I was having a conversation with the president of a college and he said, "We've got to rethink that we stop learning when we're 22 and we finish college." Who thought that was when we were supposed to stop learning? We've got to constantly be learning and surround ourselves with that nice group of people who can lift us up, encourage us, and push us out of our comfort zone. It's what separates people like you and Troy from everyone else who is trying to do it the way it's always been done. I think that's fun and interesting. How can people follow you and get in touch? How can they see what all this is about? I hope there's a YouTube channel or something with all these videos and all this stuff. How can people follow along, get in touch, and keep in touch with you?

DS: We are going to start doing more YouTube but for now, you can go to Instagram and it's easy. It's @DeniseSellsOklahoma and then we have a joint Facebook. We're joined at the hip. We're together 24/7. It's Troy Denise Schroder. I would love to connect and see if I can help anyone. I love hearing from people after listening to podcasts. That would be great.

JO: We appreciate this conversation. I'm fired up to bring some of these ideas to our people and change the way that we're thinking about how we care and love on our people and find their stories and tell their stories and make them feel they're a part of something totally special. You've inspired me. I hope you've inspired some other people and I appreciate the conversation.

Thanks so much.

—

I truly love that interview with Denise and the conversation that we had and hearing the ridiculous stories that they're doing for their clients like singing at their clients' funerals, weddings and being a part of their bridal showers and baby showers. This idea of doing things for people because they're people. She said it like, "I do these things for my friends. Why wouldn't I do them for my clients and for my customers?" As I was going back through and making notes and sharing some with our team, I was like, "Why don't we have a Red Carpet Club? Why don't we do dance and dash? Why don't we dress them in cheerleader costumes?" It was powerful. The two things that I took away as we were having that conversation and as I get back to it is she said, "If it's a big deal to our client, it's a big deal to us."

I think about all the mundane, monotonous, and typical things that we do on a business day. Do we even realize how big of a deal they are to our customers, our fans, and our clients? She was using the example of an appraisal, which I'm sure is a boring thing to deliver to someone in the real estate market. She said, "What if we dress up in cheerleader costumes and send it over to them?" That is remarkable. The question that we often get as well was, "I'm in this business and we shouldn't have fun or I'm in this business, people might be thrown off if we play jokes and if we have too much fun." She said it perfectly that if you are doing things well as an expert in your business, you have earned the right to inject joy into someone else's life. They do serious work. They take care of serious business transactions and they do it well.

READY, OK! CHEERLEADER APPRAISAL WITH THE
SCHRODER SPARTAN CHEERLEADERS

She said that sometimes there are bumps in the road. Sometimes it gets difficult. Sometimes it's a difficult conversation that you have to have with people. At the end of the day, their mission is to inject joy in people's lives and that comes through real estate. If you're questioning whether or not you feel like you can do something out of the box, funny or different, remember you're doing your business well. Don't feel bad because you have permission to inject joy into people's lives. Thanks for reading this blog. Thanks for always hanging out with us. If you have any other questions, you can always get in touch with us. Go to BananasForBusiness.com.

The show notes are a great place for the host to insert your social media handles and how and where to contact you. Build your following and future clientele through podcast guesting. It is such a fun way to expand your reach from the comfort of your own home!

When I was being tagged and read the blog Jared wrote after my podcast, it was so gratifying. To say I felt seen by this podcast host, Jared Orton, would be a gross understatement. The mere fact that one of the podcast world's most creative organizations felt inspired enough to actively tell everyone about our conversation and would bring some of my ideas to their Ideapalooza meeting to implement at their baseball stadium was out-of-the-world exciting! I want this to truly anchor with you the magnitude of podcast guesting.

> I've learned that
> people will forget what you've said,
> people will forget what you did,
> but they will never forget the
> way you made them *feel*.
> - Maya Angelou

If you ever doubt that your story is omnipotent, read the introduction descriptions the podcast host copy uses to promote the show.

When I am having a bad day, experiencing writer's block, or simply feeling burnout, I read reviews and these introductions to the podcasts I have been on. Reading and seeing my story through the eyes of others' perceptions, vocalizing how important and influential you are, brings it back full circle. We have to remember our WHY. When it is God, it flows; when it is you, it is forced.

From the podcast, Say What!? with Lady Alex

"Overcoming other people doubting you"

On this Episode, Lady Alex interviews a nationally ranked Real Estate guru out of OKC. A Top 1% earner and one half of a duo husband and wife Realtor team, this little lady has a unique vision that has helped her overcome a lot of other people doubting her, used that doubt as fuel and set herself on fire!

Last night's episode, you guys!!!!

I can't even believe how amazing this lady is! And I got to interview her and become friends with her!!!

Be sure to listen to the latest episode of the Say What!? with Lady Alex podcast and hear how Ms. Troy Denise Schroder overcame life's biggest struggle: overcoming other people doubting you!

She managed to escape a negative relationship only to be grief stricken with the loss of a parent, and yet this magical soul pulled herself from the ashes and relit that fire in her belly to succeed better and brighter than ever before!

From the podcast, Fearless Pursuits, by Sharon Lee

Denise Schroder shares her journey of delayed blessings. She shares her story of wanting to be a realtor and how someone very close to her squashed those dreams. She talks about falling in love with the FedEx guy in her office, but they did not start dating for five years. She talks about the challenges of combining their families, starting their own business, and ultimately realizing her dream of becoming a realtor. She shares how they created a business together that has morphed over time and has become incredibly successful. We cover following the little glimmers that come in, that we all have a gift to give and can all make an impact.

There is so much greatness in this episode! I wanted to share the cliff notes of these three podcasts to show you the depth of my story that shined through a short conversation. Not to mention the relationships formed and mass numbers of listeners to elevate my reach of impact!

Below is a tool I use called the 1-3-5. It is a Keller Williams tool that I love. It really helps me to drill down about my goals and then breaks each category down further. When I put things in a granular format, I can easily propel myself into doing the actionable steps to meet the goal. When I don't break these lofty goals down, it becomes really overwhelming for me. I don't know about you, but I cannot eat an elephant whole, I have to take one bite at a time. This process makes everything seem so achievable and less daunting. The last thing you want is to be that person who has a notebook full of ideas that are never brought to fruition because you throw your hands up and run like the wind due to a paralyzing fear that you just can't attack it and succeed.

1-3-5 Goal Setting Template

The One Main Goal

The Three Priorities to Achieve That Goal

5 Strategies for Completing Each Priority

1-3-5

What is my message?

Why is it helpful to others?

How can I make a difference?

How can my testimony and message move others into action?

Chapter 28
The Stage is Bare and waiting for YOU!

I have always known I had the gift of oration. It must be true, Oprah Winfrey and her staff told me so. No, really, not kidding! I have gone through a lot of frogs to get to my prince, and had rock bottom defeats, trials, rejections, abandonment, and hopelessness that I would not wish on a worst enemy. I have experienced the great loss of my mother taken too soon at age fifty from a mere misdiagnosis and delayed trip to the physician, as well as an earth-shattering divorce. I simply had to rebuild, rewire, reprogram, recharge, and reintroduce myself once I had done some healing to sort out recapturing my identity. You may be unrecognizable to yourself now, but you can come back stronger and with more clarity for what you want than ever before! All the things I trudged through, fought for, and battled for make me more qualified to infuse light and hope in others walking difficult paths. (I copied this from a post I wrote on someone's Facebook wall). I am living proof.

I have been asked to speak on many panels and speak/teach at local events. In 2020, one of my goals and focuses was podcast guesting. Podcast guesting is an incredible tool to level up and perfect your public speaking game from the comfort of your own home. However, podcast guesting was playing it safe. I am not a dip-your-toe kind of girl! I did not want to grow complacent and hide behind podcast guesting! I am always looking for the next challenge. Starting my own podcast may come later. You see, I am very time broke. The thought of the start-up process was not something I could invest energy in at this time. Podcast guesting is something I found I can easily do from my own home. The benefits are astounding. We are in a social distancing quarantine right now in my area. We were going to join Toastmasters but that is not possible right now due to the virus risks. I have found many resourceful Facebook groups that are always seeking guests with a powerful story. You can check the box for the fact that I have a unique story that inspires, stirs, and empowers others to take an audit of their life and use adversity to push through. My hope is that my story allows someone to think big, dream bigger, and believe in themselves.

PANEL INTERVIEW WITH OKLAHOMA CITY
METROPOLITAN ASSOCIATION OF REALTORS

OKLAHOMA STATE CAPITOL

A few of the messages I want to impart to anyone who will listen:

*Surround yourself with people that challenge, support and encourage you.

*Don't let anyone EVER tell you that you can't do something!

*Choose people who choose YOU!

*Wake up with a fire in your belly!

*Love and serve others the way you would serve your mama! The business will come when your heart is in the right place, and you are keen at your job!

*Without hard work, nothing grows but weeds.

*Do whatever it takes!

*If you are willing to be vulnerable, your failures actually give you credibility. Sharing your story about rising from the ashes allows you to be a lighthouse to others.

*Have a mentor and coach, also mentor others.

*Serve like you are chosen!

*Give God the glory for allowing you to minister through your work, no matter what it is.

I am just a girl chasing her dreams and having an amazing adventure.

If you could speak on a topic for thirty minutes with little to no notice, what would it be? What are you passionate about, that truly lights you up like a Christmas tree?

As mentioned in the podcast chapter, I created a speaker one-sheet to bullet-point my topics, list my experience, and provide an overview of my bio. This is a great resource to have ready when you are initiating getting a speaking gig or you would like to be a guest on a podcast. To level up, have a demo, sizzle reel created to also send out for an even better opportunity to be booked. A sizzle video reel just may be the most powerful branding tool that your business has ever had. A sizzle reel is also known as a demo reel, a public relations video, and a promo. This is a short video, usually no more than five minutes in length, which is used to get a message across about your business's brand. Giving the booking agent a perfectly packaged audiovisual representation helps them expeditiously decipher if you are a fit for the event.

Public speaking is a great way to develop some brand recognition and be viewed as an expert in the topics you speak about. If you have a book, tangible products, service, etc., it is a great platform to sell and grow your business. The last time I spoke, there were about 150 people in the room. I love that there were a lot of open ears and hearts listening to my message in person. I get to potentially build relationships stemming from us connecting at this event. My goal when I speak is to move people. I want to stir and awaken dreams, inspire ideas, and propel you into action. If I can move or impact ONE person to leap, it is a good day. I was there for that ONE person. The key in sharing your message is not being afraid to be vulnerable. The rock bottom moments and dips in your story make your rise even more beautiful. If you are like me, your rise-up muscles are strong. I have fallen more times than I can count. The lessons in my failures have made me who I am today, and I have vowed to spend the rest of my life helping others feel less broken. Don't ever let a failure or defeat prevent you from seeing the lesson. Learning and growing from your defeats will elevate you to never repeat mistakes. When we don't take the opportunity to look at our failures on a granular scale, it is a failure. When we dissect the results that were not fruitful and extract the lessons, though sometimes harsh, we come out stronger and wiser. Failure is a tremendous teacher, not a grave digger. You can't just share your story and message, you have to show your story, really peel back the layers so people can see more than your suit, perfectly groomed hair, and polished shoes.

Get laser focused on who your audience is, choose a target. Mine may be realtors all over the world and my back-up may be small business owners or women business owners. Once you choose a target, what can you feed them that they will crave? Find a void and fill it! What will keep them from scrolling Facebook, squirming in their seat, checking their clock, but will keep them focused and entranced on the message you are trying to share?

Start out by volunteering to speak at local organizations. They are always looking for speakers. Contact the local rotary, chamber of commerce, women's and mom's clubs, networking groups, Facebook groups, etc. The value you receive from volunteering at these events is incredible. What a gift and a great donation to give back to your community by volunteering your time and talent to share what you've learned. After speaking at one of the local realtor organization's meetings, I was asked if I would be open to doing coaching in the future. This is a seed planted for when our coaching business gets off the ground. I also offered to take a lucky winner of a drawing to lunch and mastermind around anything they wanted. You will begin to be recognized as a speaker and more opportunities will stem organically. You can work up to charging and working with a coach to be submitted for opportunities and directories for booking agents for events to view in one place. There are so many speaker directories and coaches to guide you in learning this lane and implementing this into your business plan to reach unlimited audiences.

My goal is to motivate others into movement and action. I have met so many people with dormant, or worse yet, aborted dreams. I hear so often that their ship has sailed, or they have allowed fear to overtake their vision of opportunities. The more you speak, the more comfortable it will become. Public speaking is a muscle many of us have never used at a high level. If you don't have Toast Masters or a coach, go on YouTube. There are many videos and Ted Talks on public speaking you can utilize for free. Personally, the mirror is my best friend when preparing to speak. It feels so foreign and weird to watch myself and keep on track with a timer, but it is imperative. You can also train yourself by starting out small with a short video. Continually work your way up to be able to give a twenty-to-forty-five-minute talk or speech. You don't start out running five miles when your feet have never stepped foot on a treadmill. It is a progressive process and practice makes perfect!

Plant Seeds

Speaking to students and seeing a light within them when your message resonates is quite surreal. Have you ever heard the saying, "If you want to truly master something, teach it"? High achievers are always stretching themselves. You've got this!

One of my favorite quotes is from John F Kennedy: "Leadership and learning are indispensable to each other."

One of the first teaching experiences we had was at Yukon High School for a finance class for seniors. I have to confess, I was nervous. I was thinking these students could be tough critics and not want to hear the knowledge and wisdom we so wanted to share. That limiting belief was so off base. When you command the presence of a room or stage with your ferocious passion, teaching and leading with a servant's heart, big things happen! You can make an impact like you never realized. If just one student has an impactful takeaway it is well worth it! Since then, we have been asked to teach for career day at middle schools and for a leadership class at a local university.

YUKON HIGH SCHOOL TEACHING INVESTING AND HOME BUYING EDUCATION

Teaching and sharing are like oxygen. There is something so fulfilling about pouring into the lives of the younger generation. From middle school up to the college level, there are always students who show such promise and that is so exciting to me.

Our topics are typically pertaining to overcoming obstacles, real estate, leadership, and personal development. We always stress the importance for the students to seek out mentors in the areas of work they are interested in. Our teaching also always illustrates some aspect of how we overcame adversity in our journey. We want to inspire and empower young people to pursue their dreams. I have learned firsthand that no dream is too big, and no dreamer is too small. And… it is never too late. Mentorship is an invaluable resource that we all need in our lives.

When we teach at a school or organization, I write a human-interest story for submission to the local newspaper publications. We have always had our articles submitted about teaching at the schools. Positive content and attention to our school systems is welcome. The teachers who booked us to speak love it too, because it brings a positive highlight on their efforts to inspire the students to think big and that no dream is too big.

The opportunities to teach are endless. You can contact every school in your area. You can speak at a general career day or a business or leadership class. Educators are always welcoming successful people to come pour into their students.

Seek out local schools where you can volunteer to teach.

What is holding you back from teaching others what your gifts and strengths are?

P.S. If your naughty inside voice is chanting and banging obnoxious tambourines in your head, "Not my circus, not my monkeys." MUTE it! All negative self-dialogue should be evicted! We all have a message and a story. You just have to drill down on who your audience is.

Just today, an Instagram notification window popped up on my screen. It shockingly said Bananas for Business was quoting me! It was some text from our podcast interview with one of the most creative and innovative companies in the world followed by a sound bite clip. Was I seeing things? Really? Not only do I have a message, but I have also inspired leaders to quote and refer to our podcast to further our reach and impact. This really meant more to me than I can humanly describe. It validates so much of the path I am on. It is definitely a marathon, not a sprint. The sprinkles of encouragement certainly substantiate my mission to write, speak, and teach beyond serving families as they buy and sell real estate.

Start saying YES. There is no opportunity too small to hone your craft while making an impact in a deeper way than you thought possible!

The Successful Speaker, a book by Grant Baldwin with Jeff Goins, is fantastic. Grant also has a podcast called The Speaker Lab. He says to focus on being the best steak, not a buffet. Home in on your topic and your lane and drill down!

What is your story?

Don't underestimate that you have one worth sharing.

What is your message?

What is your brand?

How can you make a difference today?

Can you give others actionable steps to take after hearing you speak?

You just have to be brave enough to just take the first step!

Chapter 29
Dips that Drive You

Purpose in Pain can be beautiful and fruitful. Pain can actually be a GPS to a divine purpose and greater calling on your life. I am going to dare to say the "D" word. Have you been divorced? I would not wish it on my worst enemy. I felt lost, angry, depressed, lonely, frightened, insecure, and relieved at times, to name a few emotions. I would go from one moment feeling happy about it, knowing it was for the best, to mourning our life, our home, and our kids not having both of us under one roof. A staggering statistic of nearly fifty percent of the population have gone through this struggle. And if not, you must know someone that has gone through a divorce. If you are in the rarer percentile, you had a peaceful, amicable divorce and you are still BFF's, raising children like you are business partners together. However, for the masses, no break is necessarily a good break.

Just because you are legally or physically separated does not mean the communication dwindles. There are even more issues at hand involving kids, splitting personal property, bills, etc. We have seen it all. We have witnessed sabotaging tactics to keep the marital home from selling. The parties usually are not in the same headspace. One party wants to sell, initiated the split, and has emotionally moved on. The other party oftentimes wants to keep the house, despite court orders or financial ability to stay. We are supposed to step in and get two people to agree and sign off on things when they are not on the same page or even in the same book. Our normal clients are unified when we meet to sign listing paperwork. They both want the same thing; everyone is on the same team and the same page. That is not always the case in a divorce situation. You are often the middleman who must remain neutral, or you lose credibility and trust. Once that happens, everything can easily unravel into a nasty mess with you in the middle.

I was privileged to meet Laurel Starks, author of *The House Matters in Divorce: Untangling the Legal, Financial and Emotional Ties Before You Sign on the Dotted Line*. The book is about her experience in working in family law cases and becoming a trailblazer of the divorce real estate niche. I was enamored by her drive to be nothing short of a barrier breaker and pioneer.

The book was born out of need and seeing a gap between the family law community and the real estate industry.

She began a movement in LA County to be appointed to cases to be the real estate expert and get the house sold by court appointment.

I read the book and a passion stirred inside of me that I could not deny. It did more than strike a chord. I had gone through an acrimonious divorce and custody battle that cost me over $50,000. This was my cue when I looked back over some horrific, dark times in my life that would bear fruit. This is where I realized there is purpose in pain. When you truly learn lessons from the trials, you can actually see praise in pain. Laurel is a genius in the way she breaks down the process and all the entanglements surrounding the real property. This book was such a gift, one I wish I'd had to refer to when I was navigating a divorce personally. It is a quick, digestible book leaving you to move into action.

A few years ago, Laurel Starks was creating a certification to become a Certified Divorce Real Estate Expert. She interviewed us to be a part of her beta group for the class. I was absolutely honored. She was only accepting a few agents across the country. We flew to California and attended the forty-hour class taught by an elite faculty. We had Laurel, three seasoned family law attorneys, a judge, and an expert mortgage lender. This was an overload of information I will forever refer to and carry with me in my arsenal.

When people are going through a divorce, they have so many things drastically changing in their lives. Getting divorced is hard enough, telling your kids you have to sell your family home, splitting personal property, oftentimes operating two households that used to operate as one; all of it is a strain. Where are you going to go? Do you also need to go find a job outside the home to make ends meet? People do crazy things. One party will refuse showings, damage the property to make it less desirable, refuse to even attempt to negotiate offers, or completely ghost everyone involved. That is where we come in as highly skilled conflict diffusers to keep everyone and everything on track.

We got a call from a wife who was staying in the home until the property was sold. Her husband still had controls on an app to her thermostat. When he was over at the house stopping by to quickly gather some items, he placed feces in the vents. Then he proceeded to turn the heat on high the whole day from the app on his phone while the wife was at work. Can you imagine the absolute horror? She could not figure out where the smell was coming from; it was in so many vents. It seemed the odor was seeping through the walls. She began cutting places in the sheetrock open. This smell could greatly affect the value of the house. This caused a delay in showings and was costly to mitigate the odor. We are oftentimes the first call, not the attorneys, because it directly involves the home. This was a situation to address with the attorneys when a party is destroying or wasting the asset and potentially pulling out all the stops of blocking the sale while simultaneously causing the other party a massive amount of stress.

Not to sound like a broken record, but this is true! Do you see how something so terrible in my previous years leads me to want to bless others to walk through it as painlessly and smoothly as possible? Remember when I told you God has used our tragedies, great disappointments, failures, and dips in life to qualify us to serve others. I can sit and close my eyes and take an emotional journey of what I went through in my divorce with my kids' father. I was feeling hopeless. I could barely get through the day, but yet I was expected to push through and find myself, to create a new life and identity, to be independent and self-sufficient. I was petrified I would not be able to provide for my kids. I honestly did not know how to step into the role of breadwinner, head of household in all aspects. I was really scared and yet did not have a choice. Though it may seem diabolical, I actually donated my eggs for money out of desperation to create a nest egg to move forward in my life. I gave myself shots multiple times a day to prepare for the donation process for over six weeks. I was bruised from the injections, hormones going absolutely insane, and I was an emotional wreck. I had immediately gone and gotten a job at a nearby women's hospital. I was hired as an administrative assistant for the unit, but then phased to the position of O.B. surgical technologist. This was a tough transition, but I was embraced by this staff. Although they did not know everything, they were meeting me when I was at my worst. I was at the bottom of the barrel, rock bottom. I felt brave, strong but yet broken all at once. I thrived at this job, and I know I was surrounded by so many independent women for a reason. I was inspired and it ignited a fight in me that I COULD make it. This niche' and certification is in line with my mission to spend the rest of my life making other people feel less broken.

Thus, our certification as divorce real estate experts was, again, another opportunity for a press release.

Realtor couple certified as divorce real estate experts

by RICHARD MIZE

Published: Sat, June 30, 2018, 5:00 AM

Troy and Denise Schroder, Realtors, are shown on the campus at Pomona College in Claremont, California, where earlier this year they studied family law and divorce as they relate to real estate. [PHOTO PROVIDED]

The new Divorce Real Estate Institute has recognized Troy and Denise Schroder, agents with Keller Williams Realty Elite, 5629 N Classen Blvd., as Certified Divorce Real Estate Experts.

The Schroders recently graduated from the institute's inaugural Master Course at Pomona College in Claremont, California.

The training was the first formal education on the subject of its kind in the real estate business, said Laurel Starks, founder and CEO of the institute, based in Safety Harbor, Florida. She started the institute in January.

"There's been such a disconnect between the family law profession and the real estate community," Starks said. "It's important that we as Realtors bring our tools and knowledge to the family law community as experts and professionals in our field."

The Schroders received 40 hours of in-person education, observed family court, took a 10-hour online divorce real estate principles course, as well as a 12-week learning lab conducted by attorneys, a family court judge, and a certified divorce lending specialist, all of whom serve on DREI's faculty alongside Starks.

"Divorce listings are so different," said Starks, author of "The House Matters in Divorce." "The family law community needs more real estate agents who are trained and versed in family law to minimize conflict, maximize profits, and to do it from a fair, unbiased place."

The Schroder Group at Keller Williams Elite, 5629 N Classen Blvd., has sold nearly 400 homes in the past five years, about $70 million in real estate. Trailblazing a path in family law came with a conviction to help others, Denise Schroder said.

"Divorce listings are different. We have a streamlined process establishing us as a neutral party to keep the transaction from derailing with all the emotional chaos going on," she said. "We feel called, after going through divorces of our own, to help others navigate through this period and protect the clients' equity."

Professionals in family law need fellow professionals in real estate, she said.

"Oftentimes, the family law community turns to Zillow, Redfin or the county assessor to determine values, which are not accurate or realistic oftentimes," she said.

Bridging the gap between family law and real estate "is not for the faint of heart, but it is desperately needed," she said.

Part of the training is preparation for conflict and resolution.

"We meticulously document to be prepared for court-ready reports or testimony," Denise Schroder said. "We have expectations clearly defined with the clients on an escalation process if one spouse or the other is uncooperative and blocking or hindering the sale. This happens all the time."

Only a relatively few agents have ventured into divorce real estate, she said.

"No one else (in Oklahoma City) has the designation," she said. "We were selected out of 18 agents around the country to be a part of the beta group. You have to be selected to take the program, and it is a large financial investment.

"It is for people truly convicted. We have had great success, consistently in the top 1 percent, but helping others navigate this path is a conviction. Normal familial sales are a lot easier. We are up to the challenge."

— Denise Schroder

We have always had a heavy number of clients hire us due to a divorce. I have the deepest empathy for others on this journey. I know how the house is attached to so many emotions and heartstrings. Putting a for sale sign in a yard leaves the homeowners feeling like their whole life is on display and for sale. When we deal with divorcing couples, it is inevitable that one does not want the divorce. One spouse may exhibit aggressive, oppositional behavior or just seem paralyzed, unable to move through the process on their own. Our job is to step in and exhibit an understanding of how the family law and real estate worlds intersect. We have a tailored plan to protect the sellers' net while maintaining a neutral position with both parties. We have a clearly communicated escalation process we adhere to if the transaction derails by fault of either party. We are the house's advocate, ensuring we get top dollar.

When I was selling my personal home after my divorce, I had hired a top real estate team. They were not able to take some additional safety measures I needed put into place for showings. For this reason, I released them.

That is when Wanda came into my life. She was a realtor who my aunt recommended to me. She was truly a Godsend. She might as well have had angel wings and a halo. She had years of experience, keen negotiating skills, but mostly, she was kind and nurturing. She got the house sold in ten days in August. This is not the prime time to sell in our area. She was arm in arm with me throughout the whole process. She knew I had lost my mother, my marriage, and was balancing working a mix of day and night shifts. I was exhausted from my sleep schedule being so wacky, but the emotional exhaustion was worse. I did NOT try to negotiate Wanda's commission. When we got to the closing table, I got an extra one percent of profit I was not expecting. She said she wanted to do this for me and was truly wanting the best for me. To say "my cup runneth over" was an understatement. After I had seen the difference between the two realtors, I regretted even more not getting my license. Wanda took care of business, but she was also full of wisdom, compassion, and willingness to provide a listening ear because she cared and wanted to make a difference. In 2013, my very first cross-sale was with none other than the great Wanda. We had shown buyers the house from our Craigslist ad before the Open House. They said they loved it and wanted to make an offer and were not working with a realtor. About an hour later, we got a call from a realtor stating she knew the clients' parents and she would represent them after we had procured the buyer, etc. It was really disappointing, but I was elated that Wanda would be receiving the commission. I saw it as an opportunity to come full circle, seeing blessings come back to Wanda.

Going through my experience untangling all the chaos, hurt, and financial strain surrounding selling my home gave me the stirring to help others navigate this in the best way possible.

You may ask yourself why in the world you would want to get involved with divorcing couples at a high level. Isn't it more stress, more work? Yes, it is much more time consuming. It is not for the faint of heart and it is not ambulance chasing. You are having to hold separate appointments to communicate individually and keep everyone's eye laser-focused on getting top dollar for the home. The parties are in an emotional hell. This is when they need help the most.

It is so much more gratifying when you can help a couple walk through the process as productively and peacefully as possible.

Troy and I took it a step further and made a sizable investment to obtain our Family and Divorce Mediators certification. We did this in an effort to elevate our conflict resolution skills and keep refining our ability to effectively help people. It is important to never outgrow being a student. We are constantly seeking out new areas to expand while remaining laser focused on our niche as well.

We had gotten a call from one of our preferred family law attorneys. He said he wanted us to evaluate a situation for one of his clients. He mentioned one of the partners had already called the client's lender and it may just be better to let the house go back to the bank. I told the attorney I would discuss all the options with the sellers and get back to him. The client, Maria, called me. She was out of sorts, to say the least. She had a hard time getting through a sentence without bursting into tears, which led to a bunch of words I could not understand due to her extreme state of shock and hysteria. I told her to take her time. She composed herself and settled down a bit, and finally was able to tell me her story. Her entire life had blown up in a matter of minutes. The local police had come to her door and arrested her husband, confiscated their electronic devices, and DHS took custody of her precious two-year old son. She found out that her husband was running a child pornography club through Dropbox. Dropbox alerted the authorities and he got busted. In a sweep of a few minutes, her world was shattered. I struggled to hold myself together and keep my voice from shaking. She called me to be her solution, not feel sorry for her. Troy and I had an opportunity to be her saving grace. She explained her heart was broken and she had flown out the door, gotten in her van, and had not returned to the house. She knew DHS was going to be transporting her baby to some family in another state. She had quickly thrown as many belongings as she could stack in her vehicle and got on the road. As I listened to her, I got a lump in my throat. I knew telling me this story was hard enough. I wanted to carefully choose my words because this woman was hanging by a thread. We told her we would quickly go assess the property, do the research, and get back to her. She had not a penny to her name to even pay a house cleaner, mover, or to do needed repairs to the place.

We went to the property, and I remember it like it was yesterday. It was my birthday, and it was not initially our plan to take over this task. When we walked in the house, it was a nightmare. It was in complete disarray. There was a dusting of cat litter on all the carpet throughout the house, it was so dirty. Oftentimes, the house looks like a reflection of the situation. This was true in this case. You could tell Maria was in survival mode. Things were strewn all over the house. It looked like it had been literally ransacked. The house was full of furniture and the garage was stacked with junk and trash. This was going to be a huge undertaking for us to get this home prepared for the market. We spent several hours moving all the small things into the garage, then took the trash to the curb. We offered to try to help Maria sell some of the existing furniture. Again, this is not normal behavior for a listing agent. She had literally no money or resources and my heartstrings were pulled. Every bit of her energy was getting through the investigation on her to ensure she knew nothing about her husband's activities. Maria was cleared of any association and truly had no clue her husband was involved in these heinous activities. Ultimately getting her son back was her sole focus. I understood her pain and told her we would make a way to get through everything. I estimated we could sell her home quickly and hopefully profit her $5,000. It would be tight if anything came up, but she would be in the positive if we got a best-case scenario.

We paid for a deep cleaner to come in, sold some of her furniture items, and got the house listed. She was very adamant that she wanted to avoid foreclosure at all costs. She needed to start fresh, and her main focus was being able to get her son enrolled in a good preschool. Let's just say this, I was invested and determined to meet that goal for her. We were able to sell her home in one day for top dollar with multiple offers. For the four weeks we were under contract, I was secretly a basket case and on my knees in prayer. I could not have any hiccups, like major repairs that needed to be done to hold the deal together. There was no room for error or mishaps. During the transaction, we had to wait for Maria's husband to sign the divorce papers and a quit claim deed. This was a delay that made me nervous. We were at the mercy of the courts transporting Maria's husband to the courthouse to sign. We were told he was being a bit combative over signing as well, which did not help matters. We did not want to have to go to the buyers and tell them we could not close on time. I could not afford for these buyers to back out. We got the documents signed and closed on time only by the grace of God. We were able to help Maria net over $8,000, and took care of emptying, setting out donations, as well as selling the house and furniture for her. Maria thanked me countless times. She was so gracious even though she was in full crisis mode. She got her son back and stayed living close to her relatives a few states away from Oklahoma. She was going to use that money to start completely over, provide the needs for her son, and pay off her attorney fees. Even though we can't do this much extra work for every client, Maria was sent to me for a reason. Maria had no one, no hope, no reassurance, no money, and no clarity on why this had all come crumbling down. The attorney was happy with us. We were the hero of the situation. The firm got paid through some proceeds and the client had a nest egg to move forward with versus a foreclosure and trashed credit.

I think about Maria often to this day. She often enters my thoughts and I pray for her and her son. I sincerely hope that they are in a better place and have found strength, comfort, peace, and prosperity. It was no accident I got that phone call that day. During the course of the four weeks that I was in close, daily communication with Maria, I witnessed a change. I saw her move from being depleted to putting her mama bear armor on to plow through. She developed a sense of purpose in doing whatever it took to protect and provide for her child. I could hear it in her voice that she was fighting, not freezing or fleeing.

Staking a SOLD in one day sign is so fun. Being a part of helping a client rise up, show them this is only a season, walking arm in arm with them, going the extra mile, and empowering them to cross the finish line is so much more rewarding. And let me tell you, it warms the soul.

So, when people ask me why in the world I would want to step into a boxing ring with two fighting spouses, this is why. It is about aiding people to get through the process of selling their homes. It is not real estate, it is their home, their life. The house is a representation of everything they have experienced and built together as a family.

You may very well feel convicted about something else. Maybe you have a heart for the elderly or serving military clients. Working in this niche is extra stress and a lot more work. For us personally, it is gratifying in a way that feels more like a ministry than a business. To me, that is what it is all about. At the end of the day, if we are doing our consistent action items to generate business, we will get sales. Laying my head on my pillow at night and feeling like I made a difference in someone's life is such a bigger reward than any status symbol or professional award.

The moral of this story is to find the purpose in your pain and pay it forward. All of the pain I personally endured through my own divorce instilled a deep sense of empathy. I now have a conviction to help others navigate this in the most peaceful way to protect their emotional well-being and their net.

I have found something I am passionate about and that I believe is worth the extra work, efforts, and fight!

Divorcing Parents Seminars

Seminars for Divorcing Parents of Minor Children

Approved By Canadian County

(Pursuant to Title 43 Section 107.2)

Calm Waters Parenting Through Divorce Seminar (405) 841-4800

Oklahoma Cooperative Extension Service Center (405) 262-0155

Parenting Through Divorce (405) 262-7227

Co-Parenting Beyond Divorce (405) 306-0108

Chapter 30
Lights, Camera, Story

It sounds crazy to say but my adult life has literally been chronicled on national television. How cool is that? I always say I am "almost famous." I am a serial reality TV personality!

I mentioned earlier that my first story submission was to HARPO Studios for the Oprah Winfrey Show. Go BIG or go home, I always say. After being the focal point of the episode and invited back six months later to do a follow-up show, I was confident story-showing was a gift I could use in a massive way. So that is what I have done. My experience was awesome! The director flew to our home and taped us for eight hours to build our story. We were flown there and spent time with a few authors of two different books that were featured as expert physicians and specialists on the show who covered the topic well. We got to go to the show right after we filmed, and guess who we went to see. Chris Rock! What a fantastic episode to be a part of and an unforgettable experience!

NBC STUDIOS TO SHOOT MY FIRST EPISODE ON THE
STEVE HARVEY SHOW

STEVE HARVEY DRESSING ROOM SHOT WITH
PRODUCER

SPEAKING ON THE DANGERS OF TEEN TECHNOLOGY

The second opportunity was to be featured for a segment with Steve Harvey, along with Holly and Rodney Peete. The segment was my wheelhouse. The topic was Dangers of Teen Technology. I was equipped to educate the world on some of the spookiest and most dangerous apps for children. With five teenagers, we felt like we were part-time private investigators just trying to keep everyone safe. We had grown alarmed when Snapchat came out, as well as an app called Omegle, a stranger app. I was able to clearly articulate my conviction on the danger of this app to a large audience. More than one of the kids had this app on their device. Omegle is a stranger app platform. The problem is our youngest did not realize that she was most likely chatting with men old enough to be her father posing as pre-teens. Upon discovering this, we were disturbed. This was just one of the apps that we discussed among many things that were frightening, to say the least, as a parent. My mission was to awaken parents that it is our responsibility to monitor electronic devices and apps our children are accessing. Our youngest was just naive. She could have easily fallen into a trap of divulging location, contact information, and even agreed to a face-to-face meeting, God forbid. Our daughter was mortified. I was going on national TV to discuss these dangers and our grave concerns. We were able to reach so many with Steve Harvey's viewership.

THE STEVE HARVEY SHOW BLENDED FAMILY EXPERT SHOW

The third opportunity was to be featured on *The Steve Harvey Show* as blended family experts. This was an incredible adventure. We had received an email about this topic needing experts just a few months after my prior appearance. I responded and then received further instructions about doing a video explaining our story. Soon after, we had a Skype audition call with a casting director. We were immediately notified they wanted us on the show. It is always a whirlwind with these shows. We got word we would fly out twenty-four hours later. The producer sent us our flight confirmation and told us a car would be picking us up at the airport. The staff know how to make you feel famous. I can remember the production staff and assistants all going above and beyond to ensure we were spoiled rotten from the moment we stepped off the airplane. When we arrived at NBC Studios, we were whisked away to our own personal green room. I was greeted with a wardrobe specialist who came in and offered to do an emergency hem job on Troy's suit pants. I was taken to a room floor to ceiling full of beautiful clothes. I was told to pick out anything my heart desired and then come out so they could assess and help pick out the "IT" ensemble. After I picked out my outfit, I was taken to hair and make-up! I was in hog heaven! I had a make-up artist working on me while the stylist was doing my hair. Every person I came in contact with was so joyful and led with a servant's heart. After I was powdered, pressed, and curled, I was led back to the green room. Steve was coming offstage after the episode he was filming just wrapped. He had tears coming down his face, but he said hello and that we were going to have a great show! I found out he had just filmed his first intervention type show with Dr. Drew. They all thought the young man was going to accept the offer to be sent to drug treatment on Steve's dime. At the last minute before the episode concluded, the addict said he changed his mind and did not want any help. Steve was visibly shaken by this, and it was a rare, vulnerable moment. I had always been a fan of his, but even more so now.

A producer came in to ask us questions and go over our material we would be discussing during the show. She wanted to make sure we were ready to clearly and concisely convey our message in a silver-tongued fashion. We then met the other couples on the panel and went over our material. There were four couples, and we were the only blended family representatives. We were able to give some advice to a newly blended family who was really struggling with disciplining all the children equally. It is hard enough to join and mesh children. You change their birth orders when you blend, and it can be a circus. All the kids transition at a different pace and meeting the children where they are in their journey to acclimate is imperative. They are all so different. Troy and I blended five kids; four girls and one boy, which was a challenge, to say the least. Our biggest advice is to always be a united front. Whether or not you disagree. Go behind closed doors to discuss anything not unified. The kids will do their best to divide and conquer if they smell inconsistency and disunity. Setting that boundary early on is key to establishing an even playing field and doing your best to discipline equally. They are all watching how the other kids are being disciplined with an eagle eye! We survived raising all five teenagers and are living to tell about it!

Steve opened up the segment and introduced us as blended family experts who quit their jobs to become real estate agents. Did you just hear that? STEVE HARVEY gave a snippet of our story as an introduction. This statement was incredible! How often can you get Steve Harvey to mention your profession when you are on the show for a completely different personal topic? We spliced his introduction and used it in a marketing video we made. It is not every day Steve Harvey is introducing you in a way you can repurpose and use in your marketing content. It was GOLD!

Our first episode on HGTV's *House Hunters* aired in 2014. It was an even sweeter accomplishment because many had warned me that Oklahoma is not coastal or interesting enough to draw the show here. This negative noise only set me in my propel-beast mode. After I spoke at our national convention for Keller Williams in 2013 on marketing homes, an agent approached me. She told me she was featured on an episode of *House Hunters*, and I would be perfect. I came home from Phoenix and did my homework on auditioning. The process was more rigorous than I expected. We got instructions on multiple videos that had to be submitted perfectly. We spoke to a casting producer several times. We had the perfect buyer who was a single dad and Air Force veteran from Boston. Dominic submitted his audition tapes, and we were given full casting approval very quickly. I was so pumped to do this episode. This was a dream come true. The free, mass exposure was sure to create local brand recognition and growth. Our local newspapers all carried the story multiple times. We got published when we were first cast, again when the show was set to air, and oftentimes after it aired featuring photos from our watch party, etc.

I was able to convince an old classmate of mine to have us on his sports radio show on the Sports Animal station. This show has a large local audience. I told him real estate is a sport. We were notified that so many unexpected folks heard us on this show. Never underestimate exposure even though you may think the outlet is not your wheelhouse. We had our watch party at our home for the first episode. Troy built an eight-foot-tall by twelve-foot-wide screen for us to set up as a projector for a big screen experience. We had over one hundred people show up to support us and share in the excitement. What a surreal moment to have so many loved ones, friends, and clients show up to support one of the biggest accomplishments of all time in my life.

HGTV, HOUSE HUNTERS OKC EPISODE, 2014

It is rare for the producers to allow the realtors to also be the buyers. It is an interesting viewpoint of going on a journey to purchase a home through the lens of a realtor as the buyer. The episode was called Oklahoma's Toughest Client. That is in reference to ME! Troy showed me hundreds of homes. I am the worst buyer client EVER and everyone agreed! Troy used to trick me and say we were going on a date, and when I got in the car, there would be a generous stack of MLS sheets on the dash for our home tour.

There are usually two buyers and an agent on the show. If you are single, you bring a friend or relative to help you with the decision making. Having only two people carry the episode is a little trickier. This episode, which aired in 2017, was great, and the ratings were amazing.

HGTV, HOUSE HUNTERS OKC EPISODE, 2017

The third episode was an absolute surprise! I got a call from HGTV. The scout asked me about a gorgeous home we had listed that was under contract. He wanted to know if the buyers would be interested in doing an episode. The house was unique for anywhere in the country, much less Oklahoma.

HGTV, HOUSE HUNTERS OKC EPISODE 2019

Let me back up, there is a beautiful story I will unpack here. About ten years ago, we had a photography business. I was volunteering to photograph my daughter's eighth grade formal. We were all meeting at this home by Lake Overholser, that is an absolute famous staple property in Yukon, Oklahoma. I can distinctly remember walking up the walkway with my heavy photography backpack in tow. I looked up at this magical, magnificent Victorian home that literally choked me up inside. I can remember thinking to myself that I could never have a home like this. It just seemed surreal. I had seen the home while driving by but had never been up close or inside. From the moment you step in, you are in awe. There is an energy and magic that just makes you happy and feel at peace. The first eye-catching feature when you walk in the home is a dreamy, lush oasis backyard that leaves you feeling like you are entering a vacation resort, not a residence. The home was painted very eclectic, bright colors throughout. It matched the owners,' George and Gina's, personality to a tee. Everyone that comes to the house is enamored with the charm and uniqueness.

Fast forward five more years when we had recently started doing real estate. From the beginning of our career, I had George and Gina in our database and mailouts. They had mentioned to us that they were wanting to pursue their dream of moving to Hawaii. We got a call to look at the house and walked through. We gave them tips to neutralize and pre-pack, etc. It took nearly two years until we got THE call that they were going to choose us to list the house. I was more excited about listing this home than any other. I called it the Dollhouse! On the day before the Open House, I told Troy we needed to leave plenty early because I had a special plan. Anytime he hears me say something like this, he instantly gets frazzled. He immediately assumes that I am going to involve him in a zany marketing scheme I cooked up in this beautiful mind of mine. I told him all I needed him to do was be the photographer, so he was cool with that. I came out in my wedding dress. When I say wedding dress, I mean flowing, never-ending ruffles, and a train that is a block behind you. It is a grand, masterpiece dress fit for a princess, or me. I went to the local bridal store to pick out the dress. I went to the $100 clearance rack. It was on the wrong rack. It should have been on the DESIGNER rack. It was too late. Once I tried it on, the dress attendant had to beg me to take the dress off. I wanted to marry the dress! It made me feel like the princess I was becoming in marrying Troy. I still wear the dress to this day at any opportunity. I stood on the sidewalk with a life-size party diamond ring. I held the ring out and captioned the photo, "You'll love the house so much, you'll want to marry it! #putaringonit" I did a live video and packed the Open House with tons of traffic. Troy later started secretly negotiating a deal with the seller to buy me this house! So...WE put a ring on it!

MARRY IT!

OUR DREAM DOLLHOUSE THAT WE PUT A RING ON!

Each and every time we have been on a show, we have been featured in multiple local publications.

The moral to this story is dreams do come true. Fairytales DO happen. God blessed the broken road that led Troy and I together. This home represents a dream.

I already mentioned in a prior chapter my latest experience on season twenty of *Worst Cooks in America* on the Food Network. Each time I was featured in my on-the-fly interview segments on the show, the ticker on the screen displayed my name and my profession, REALTOR! This afforded so many media opportunities promoting the show, as well as recapping my time on the hit series. If you have a good story and you are doing big things, publicity is the gift that keeps on giving.

I have been able to use my performing, teaching, writing, and public speaking skills to marry into using TV, newspaper, radio to give us the exposure to grow at an unexplainable rate. Each and every time we have been on a show, we have been featured in multiple local publications. Free publicity has been an amazing tool we have been able to use to quickly grow name recognition and branding in our community. It has been invaluable being cast on these shows and having so much positive exposure for both ourselves and our community. At the end of the day, each and every opportunity has one common thread – story-showing! If you would have told me my adult life would be chronicled on CBS, HGTV, ABC, and the Food Network, I would have told you you're crazy! Everyone has a story, why not use your message to make a difference in the lives of others and have a broad impact, all while growing your business?

What absolutely divine timing!

Today we just got the official word that our next venture with HGTV has received the greenlight as well. We will begin working on this project next month. Relationships and connections are truly everything in any business. For the entertainment industry, when you bring the sauce and spice to your episodes and the ratings are more than favorable, the producers and directors look good to the executives.

This leads to them never forgetting you.

When we went under contract with an out of this world unique property last week, I immediately texted my favorite Director. I sent a link to the property and a photo of my buyer. I received a phone call back in merely 5 minutes. This is a man that works 60 + hours a week and travels all over the country. The expeditious response time is mind blowing. We always do our best to express and articulate our extreme gratitude to the casting staff for believing in us time and time again.

Appearing on an episode of such a monster network one time is a once in a lifetime opportunity

To be able to do this 4 times is unfathomable.

I can't help but give God all the glory for each and every opportunity.

Do you love the spotlight?

Are you a ham?

Use the power of the media to grow your business at lightning speed! Enjoy the ride!

DENISE FAWN SCHRODER

SOLD BY SCHRODER

CAST OF HOUSE HUNTERS 2019 BEHIND THE SCENES

Conclusion

As we are approaching the end of the book, I wanted to share a little bit about success and what it means to me. We all define it and measure it differently. For many years, I felt I was a loser, for lack of a better term. I felt trapped, stagnant, and worthless. I felt like surviving to collect a paycheck in a dead-end job left me intellectually unchallenged and unfulfilled, lacking all passion, hope, and purpose.

> suc·cess
>> 1.the accomplishment of an aim or purpose.
>> "The president had some success in restoring confidence"
>> 2.the attainment of popularity or profit.
>> "The success of his play"
>> 3. a person or thing that achieves desired aims or attains prosperity.
>> "I must make a success of my business."

"We cannot become what we want by remaining what we are."
—Max Depree

All those variations of definitions we had accomplished, but yet still felt void in this category. Some are out climbing the ladder, working for the title and the almighty buck. While some are searching for meaning and purpose, it is more vital to leave a legacy. That does not mean you can't do both. You can be prosperous and have a mission to help impact and change the lives of others for the better. I had to really do some deep soul searching for this one. I had to give myself permission to be proud of being prosperous and successful. I have had to learn that not everyone will grow with you. I have had friends who choose to be complacent and stationary with their lives, so they have been uncomfortable with my growth and relentless drive. There is no right or wrong. I do know that I am the average of the five people I hang with and am influenced by the most. That is my future. I have had to make difficult decisions to choose people who choose me. I have had fellow realtors, family, and friends not accept or support our passion to pursue our dreams. In the past, I have allowed others to dictate my worth, value, and career path. I am not that person any longer. That version of me has been evicted. I will continue to be kind and freely forgive, but not ask permission to be who I am. I am strong, passionate, driven and will do whatever it takes to blaze a trail and continue to propel myself into the next level of challenging myself.

One thing I have learned through this whirlwind experience is setting realistic goals on yourself. I had such a paradigm shift when I lost my mom. I did not start real estate until I was 39 years old. In my mind, I was thinking if I only have eleven more years to live like my mother, I have to hustle to achieve and prove I can do this. That mindset created a relentless grind that put an immense amount of pressure on myself. We were achieving the unthinkable and I was missing one thing. I was not stopping to savor the moment of what we had accomplished. I was quickly moving to the next goal without even enjoying monumental moments. Create margin and boundaries for your personal and business life. Real estate is something that I absolutely love, but we must prioritize and have quality time to refresh and recharge. Part of my definition of success now is creating white space and time for self-care and quality time with family and friends.

Have you been holding back due to not wanting to ruffle the feathers of the ones around you? You might consider getting a new tribe if you have outgrown the one you are in! With saying that, you can love people from afar while intentionally choosing who you spend the most time with.

If you are doing incredible, outstanding things in life, haters are just a part of the package. I am a people pleaser to the core, and this is something I work on daily. Haters don't have to be a negative thing. Haters can remind you that you are excelling and capturing enough attention that you are intimidating them. Allow that to serve as a propellant, not a hindrance to you moving to the next level.

When I first started in real estate, success to me meant something polar opposite and looked very different. We were living paycheck to paycheck, and I just wanted to get out of debt and have money to go on one incredible vacation a year. I also wanted to be a top producer. I wanted my name in lights or my sign on every block in town! After achieving our production goals, purchasing investment properties, and becoming debt free, I still did not feel successful! I still felt like I had a J-O-B with no sense of control. I did not have the leverage. I honestly did not have any quality time whatsoever. Going out or on a vacation with a preoccupied person still spewing all things real estate is not fun! I can remember while on a cruise to Alaska a few years ago, hiding in the bathroom trying to not let anyone else know I was working and putting out fires here in Oklahoma. We have since gotten leverage and it has given us a sense of our lives back, something we had forgotten existed. The power and importance of prioritizing your relationships over work is imperative. If you allow it to, real estate can swallow you whole.

I urge and challenge you to dig deep and create your own path for your authentic brand. Establish and know your audience and become a black belt in being different, be YOU! No one can replicate how uniquely and wonderfully made you are. When you live a purpose-drenched life, it changes things on a molecular level.

Today, success to me is simple. It is living and walking in my purpose to make a difference in the lives of others. This fills and overflows my cup, and I am grateful to have been given the gifts to pass onto others. Success is not my sales ranking, what others think or believe about me, or the balance of my bank account. It is the quality of loving fiercely, giving generously, and serving others ferociously to help them find their own success and reach their goals.

In the book Psychology of Money, by Morgan Housel, he shares a profound story that deeply resonated with me. At a party given by a billionaire on Shelter Island, Kurt Vonnegut informs his pal, Joseph Heller, that their host, a hedge fund manager, had made more money in a single day than Heller had earned from his wildly popular novel Catch-22 over its whole history.

Heller responds, "Yes, but I have something he will never have — ENOUGH."

Enough — What an eloquent word.

Enough — What a potent word.

Enough — An underused word, maybe.

Theodore Roosevelt once said, "Comparison is a thief of joy." I have a deep understanding that too much is given, much is required. I don't feel guilt for being prosperous or successful anymore. But I also live in a mindset of abundance. I have enough. Period.

I was intentional to change my internal soundtrack. Today my daily affirmations and internal dialogue are very different than what I wrote on page 1:

I AM EXACTLY WHERE I AM SUPPOSED TO BE

I AM LOVED AND HAVE IMMENSE VALUE

I DO HAVE WHAT IT TAKES

I AM UNIQUELY AND WONDERFULLY MADE

BEING DIFFERENT IS MY SUPERPOWER

I AM VIRTUOUS AND SALT OF THE EARTH

I AM ENOUGH

I don't just recite these to myself, I internalize them, and I BELIEVE them. Remember your mission and the legacy you want to leave behind and live it out beautifully.

Serve. Love. Forever be a student. Teach others without reservation. Have a coach and mentor and give your knowledge and resources freely! One thing I am certain of, you will be blessed bountifully.

It is never, never too late to start. We all have a story to tell, gifts inside us, and a purpose to step into. I can't wait to hear yours and share in you discovering your own lane while being creatively courageous!

"You either walk inside your story and own it, or you stand outside your story and hustle for your worthiness." –Brene' Brown

My prayer is for this to awaken your soul to crave more and propel you into action! No matter what journey you are on, always serve like you are CHOSEN and you will be taking the first step to change the world! You may just find your fairytale too.

DREAMS REALLY DO COME TRUE.

About the Author
Meet Denise Schroder

Denise is proud to be a farmer's daughter from a small town—Blackwell, Oklahoma. She has never forgotten her roots and attributes them to her ferocious work ethic. She has a laundry list of titles, Realtor, CEO, Author, Speaker, Coach and Marketing Strategist, wife, mom, and Coco to name a few. Denise has a magical way of story "showing." She is not afraid of spilling the raw footage of her life—the grit, dips, and rise—to where she is now.

She loves spending her free time with family, playing with her grandson, singing backyard karaoke, burning dinner on the stovetop (just watch her on Worst Cooks of America!), and trying her best to garden. It's a process. She also goes by the name, crazy cat lady. Yes, she spoils her fur babies to the max!

She loves to connect with her followers on social media with her Out of the Box thinking. Troy pretends to not like it but secretly, he loves every minute of everything she convinces him to do. Well, most everything.

You can find Denise hanging out on Facebook, TikTok, and Instagram.

https://www.instagram.com/denisesellsoklahoma/

https://www.facebook.com/tdschroder

tiktok.com/@troyndenise

Book Denise to speak and order Out of The Box @

WWW.DENISEANDTROY.COM

Click on MY BOOK TAB!

Please reach out to me if you enjoyed the book! I would love to hear from you personally.

Made in the USA
Middletown, DE
07 October 2022

12158994R00179